The American Journey

MONKS OF MT. TABOR

The American Journey

A Theology in the Americas working paper

Joe Holland

Published by
IDOC/North America, New York
in cooperation with
Center of Concern, Washington, D.C.

The American Journey
© 1976 by Center of Concern.
3700 13th Street, N.E., Washington, D.C. 20017.
Published by IDOC/North America, Inc.
145 East 49th Street, New York, New York 10017.
Distributed exclusively by Center of Concern.

ISBN 0-89021-035-7

Library of Congress Catalog Card Number
77-78071

Printed in the U.S.A.

Issued to subscribers only as No. 73 in the monographic series
IDOC/International Documentation
published by IDOC/North America, Inc.,
under the general editorship of
Pat VanHeel Gaughan.

Contents

For Paquita

Introduction

Throughout its history America has sparked hope across the world. Its independence revolt, its call to a democratic way of life, the resistance of its slaves, its abolitionist movement and subsequent Civil War, its feminist movement, and its dramatic labor struggles have all stirred hearts all over the world. Perhaps in no other time or place has the struggle for freedom been so dramatic and well known. And yet, in the third quarter of the 20th century, America is perceived by many in the world as an enemy of freedom. Why?

The answer is not that there *is* no longer any American struggle for freedom. At times, because of the complexity of America's social struggles, the pieces do not fit together well, but never can it be said—not even to this day—that America is a nation without struggle.

One answer may be that the structural context of America's social struggles often weakens or even undercuts the battles which are waged. It is the thesis of this essay that the *structures of American capitalism* (cultural, political, and economic) have kept the American struggles for freedom from bearing their richest fruit. This does not mean that past struggles have been in vain. It simply means that America's many, and often separate, struggles for freedom must grapple with the structural context common to them all.

Part of this thesis is the claim that there is ground for cooperative solidarity between America's ordinary people and the ordinary people of the rest of the world, because both the American people and the people of other nations are exploited and manipulated by the *integrated* structures of world (not only American) capitalism. Underlying this claim is the assertion that in a certain sense there are two Americas, namely, the America of its ordinary people (in turn racially, ethnically, and functionally diverse) and the America of the dominant social class (in turn presiding with other national elites over an international economic system). In this perspective, when voices of protest arise in the world against America, they are not condemnations of the American people but cries of protest against the transnational elites whose international structural control is founded on the exploitation of people both in this country and in other areas of the world. This perspective, then, would seek to discover how the protest of exploited people of the Third World, for instance, can be seen in solidarity with the social anger of ordinary Americans. It would seek to discover in what way the unified structures of international capitalism are felt as common forces of exploitation at home and abroad. In what sense was the economic blockade against the people of Chile under the presidency of Salvador Allende structurally related to the current economic attacks on the people of New York City? In what sense is domestic inflation and unemployment simply one expression of a global systemic crisis in world capitalism? These would be but some examples of the task presented by this thesis.

So too within the nation, according to this thesis, there is ground for cooperative solidarity among all of America's ordinary people—of all racial and ethnic backgrounds, both men and women, and across a broad range of functional stratification. What are the dynamics within each of these groupings? First, there is America's racial and ethnic pluralism, rightfully defending itself against the plastic monoculture of the melting pot, and including Native Americans whose ancestors were here for so long before the European settlers; the early European settlers, mainly English, who established the young nation; the African Americans who were brought here as slaves by the planter class; the Hispanic Americans whose land was annexed by the young empire; and the Asian and later European immigrant Americans who came with industrialization. Second, there is a difference between America's men and women, the latter waging a long and unfinished battle to have the full force of their voice heard in the land. And finally there is the functional stratification of America's workers, divided into "middle class" and "working class," into "professionals" and "paraprofessionals," into "skilled" and "unskilled," into "blue collar" and "white collar," into "productive" and "service," into "employed," "underemployed," and "unemployed"—and within all these categories, divisions into a thousand lesser forms.

Among all these groups there are important grievances still outstanding. Some have benefited from the American experiment more than others, and still others have not benefited at all. At times the success of some depends upon the failure of others. The very serious issues which keep these groups at times divided from one another are not resolved simply by pointing to their common structural environment of capitalism. Yet precisely without attention to this common structural environment, the very real issues which pit America's ordinary people one against another can be manipulated (consciously or unconsciously) by those who control the social structures. That manipulation fragments and even shatters the ground for any broad-based coalition in the American social struggle.

Worse still, it increasingly appears that no single group, particularly those who have been most oppressed in the journey, will be successful in redressing its wrongs without simultaneously challenging the structural context in which these wrongs have been generated. For much of past American history, particularly in the two decades following World War II, that did not seem to be the case. Now, however, structural developments seem to make the link inescapable. For instance, America's native peoples again find their few land holdings (the root of their culture) under attack in the rush for new energy sources. This in turn raises the question of the energy crisis itself, which compels us to examine the international structures of contemporary capitalism. So too the social struggle of minorities and women, as affirmative-action and equal-opportunity policies collapse, must come to terms with the issue of unemployment and its structural roots in contemporary American capitalism.

Because, historically, great social manipulation has been effected in America between domestic and foreign policy (and, within domestic policy, among the many competing social groupings), it is very important to develop a *holistic structural interpretation of the American struggle for freedom.* Such an interpretation would have to do justice to the integrity of each part of that struggle but also understand how they are linked together.

In attempting to take some steps toward such a holistic structural interpretation, this paper tries to recall some of the forgotten stories, or forgotten aspects of remembered stories, and to discover some points of overlap and connection. The stories center, in varying degrees, around the struggles against four fundamental, interconnected oppressions: *class exploitation, imperialism, racism,* and *sexism.* Not all elements are developed as well as they should be here. It is hoped that this paper will be taken as one limited contribution among many, each reflecting the richness and handicaps of the personal social history out of which it proceeds.

At this point it is absurd to think that any single social movement contains the whole story. Nor can any single storyteller pretend to be the architect gathering all into a masterplan. This is not only because the individual pieces of the American Journey are so complex but also because a true holistic interpretation must be the cooperative construction of people who represent all the pieces. Anything less than that would represent not a creative vision of the whole but the distasteful arrogance of a single piece.

It would be equally absurd, however, to pretend that one should deal with one's own piece and with no other. Each piece, or the story of each social group in the complex pluralism of the American Journey, contains implicitly its perspective on the whole story. This perspective in turn contains important hints about the interconnections.

An Experiment with Marxian Analysis

The main theoretical resource throughout this interpretation is Karl Marx.[1] This choice perhaps appears strange for a paper to be used by American Christians, because Marx was an atheist. Yet thinkers such as the Latin American theologian Gustavo Gutiérrez have distinguished different analytical levels of Marxism (scientific, utopian, and metaphysical) and relate to each level differently.[2] There is no question, of course, but that the metaphysical elements of atheism and mechanistic materialism which have emerged within the Marxian tradition are not compatible with Christian faith. Still the Marxian tradition is not static, and many from within it are raising questions about one or both of these elements. This opening within the Marxian tradition, as well as the development of new theological interpretations of the relation between history and the religious mystery, has enabled a minority of Christians from many parts of the world to adopt Marxist social interpretations.

The growing interest by Christians in the Marxian tradition was perhaps best symbolized by a recent address of Dom Helder Camara for the celebration of Thomas Aquinas' 700th anniversary. On that occasion, Dom Helder proposed that, were Aquinas alive today, the figure he would tackle would be Marx rather than Aristotle.[3]

The turn to Marx's thought here is only an experiment, but a serious experiment nonetheless. In testing this perspective, it seems possible to accept Marx's insights regarding social science without rejecting faith in the living God, just as Christians only a few generations ago accepted the insights of many natural scientists (or, more recently, personality scientists) for whom atheism and science were originally interwoven. Also, in testing Marx's perspective, one must realize that modern capitalism is more complex than its 19th century counterpart and that throughout its life capitalism has shown more resilience and maneuverability than Marx himself foresaw. Nonetheless, for many reasons, it still seems that an interpretation of the American experience through Marxian eyes is worth serious examination.[4]

Of course, the experiment with Marxian analysis does not mean to be blind to or to condone the many abuses and injustices which have occurred under Marx's name. One thinks especially of the cruel religious persecutions in Eastern Europe and of the general absence of a tradition of civil liberties in many socialist nations. But we can no more hold Marx accountable for all that has been done in his name than we can blame Jesus for the many sins which Christians have committed in his.

In Marx's thought, all contemporary injustice, despite deep roots even beyond human memory, are conditioned and reshaped by modern capitalism and become in turn functionally integrated sources of exploitation for that system. This is true of racism, sexism, and imperialism, as well as of classism. Within the capitalist social experience, the persistence of these oppressions in their contemporary

form must be examined in relation to the maximization of profit.
So too, the struggles against all these historical oppressions potentially
constitute a fresh historical project reaching out to a new structural
order, namely, socialism. The nature of that social order is vague and
not limited to present expressions of it. Indeed, since respect for
concreteness is theoretically important in the Marxian tradition
(there is no universal abstraction, but only a dialectic between
abstraction and concreteness), such a project in the American context
would have to be toward a specifically American socialism, drawing on
the uniqueness of the American tradition.

For the purpose of this paper, some key assumptions of Marx's
thought are understood to be the following:

(1) that societies are founded on economic modes of production,
and that each distinct mode of production operates on laws
peculiar to it, which in turn strongly condition over the long run
the political and cultural life of each society. (To say that
humans are merely economic creatures is an inaccurate
caricature of this assumption.);

(2) that injustice is generated or perpetuated mainly through social
structures which operate according to the principles of the
productive mode and which are managed by the dominant social
class; and

(3) that the historical struggle for justice grows out of
contradictions emerging within these structures.

Grappling with Social Consciousness

If the American experience is to be taken seriously from the
Marxian perspective, this will require, perhaps here more than anywhere
else, grappling with the social consciousness and the operation of culture.
Incidentally, this stress on consciousness and culture has been a strong
theme among Christians presently experimenting with Marxism. In this
regard, one of the more noteworthy theoretical resources has been the
Italian Marxist, Antonio Gramsci, and his development of the notion of
"cultural hegemony."[5]

We know that a shift in perceptions to the fundamental level
requires a massive cultural struggle with dominant forms of social
consciousness, even though the social struggle is more than cultural. In
contemporary American capitalism, social myth functions in a complex
and indirect system of rationalization, which spontaneously arises out of
the productive process itself and is later sharpened by cultural
institutions into a formal ideology encompassing attempts to legitimate
structures of injustice.

An example of this rationalization process is the American myth of
success—"Those who want to can make it"—only recently coming into
serious question. The myth locates social failure with individuals

rather than with structures in a "blame the victim" theory. Thus, if some are unemployed, it is because they are lazy and not because a flexible margin of unemployment is structurally necessary to manage an economy lacking fundamental planning, as well as to check the economic demands of organized labor. And further, for example, if many unemployed people are black, this fact is used as a demonstration of how blacks tend to be lazy, rather than how they functionally serve as a secondary labor market. Then when black unemployment produces drug addiction and crime within the black community, strong police control over black communities is legitimated. The resulting social situation requires a strong police presence and a bursting prison system, as well as a giant welfare apparatus. In turn, resentment is generated within the middle and lower-middle white sectors, from which heavy taxes are required to pay the social costs of a manipulated labor market. The spontaneous response is to place the blame with the most visible agent, namely, the black community itself, and not with the employment structure dictated by a system based on maximization of profit.

In such a complex system of legitimation, real power remains anonymous, as contrasted with earlier social systems where legitimation was directly applied to the controlling class (e.g., "noblesse oblige" or "divine right of kings"). The complexity which is evidenced in the legitimation system holds true throughout the economic and political systems of contemporary American capitalism. Confronted with such complexity, the task of critical structural analysis for the United States becomes demanding, but all the more important.

Unfortunately little work has been done in this area. A great deal of the Marxian tradition in the United States was built up and shaped by immigrant peoples whose perceptions were shaped by social struggles elsewhere. These Marxists came especially from Germany but also from Italy, Poland, Hungary, Russia, and even the Caribbean. Most recently among many Christians the interest in Marxism is coming out of international struggles, either from the anti-imperialist movement against the Vietnam war or from people with experience in Latin America. These contributions are all helpful and important, but they do not give us direct access to our own past or present experience.

The Structure of This Essay: History and Projected Scenarios

Part of the Theology in the Americas process has been to take some steps in precisely this area. "The American Journey," developed in collaboration with Mary Burke and William Ryan (originally subtitled "Toward a Critical and Constructive Analysis of the American Struggle against Class Exploitation, Imperialism, Racism, and Sexism") has three sections, the first dealing with independence and democracy in the American foundation; the second, with the period of American expansion, both outwardly in geography and internally in productivity

and in the size of the labor force (a period which covers most of American history); the third, the present period of limits and crises, with some projection of possible scenarios out of the crises.

The foundation of the United States was a period more complex than our school books tell us. Already there were strong class and racial antagonisms in the society. The American elite—merchants and traders in the northern and central Atlantic Coast and planters in the South—decided on independence because the British empire, itself shifting to industrial capitalism, began to turn harsh economic screws on the formerly comfortable colonies. Since these screws were felt by the poor, the workers, and small farmers as well as by the elites, the controlling classes were able to gather national solidarity around the independence struggle.

Structurally, however, the bid for independence had to be also a bid for a separate American empire, since the colonies were already well integrated within the world trading system of the British. Gradually in American history, the imperial side of the American experience took on racist tones and its control of new territories, markets, and labor forces was justified along ethnic lines.

But if the independence movement produced great national solidarity against the British, that solidarity was only a fragile coalition. Immediately in the postwar period there were great struggles between workers and small farmers on the one side and the controlling elites on the other. Shays' Rebellion in Massachusetts is the best-known example. This, of course, says nothing of the still deeper conflict between the Native Americans or black slaves and the rest of the society. In reaction against populist pressures, the political structuring of the society took a conservative course along the lines of a system of checks and balances which, while preventing the tyranny of a single person, also made it difficult for popular will to take institutionalized expression.

Really there were two interpretations of democracy in play, undifferentiated in the Declaration of Independence: the freedom of people and the freedom of property; but in the early Constitution the power of property gained the upper hand.

The period of expansion which followed the foundation is also rich and complex. In the course of two centuries the United States grew from a cluster of tiny colonies snuggled along the Atlantic coast to a giant nation dominating the world both militarily and economically. Territories, peoples, and markets came under the sway of the United States, either explicitly or implicitly, both by subtlety and by brute force, across the continent and throughout the world. Similarly, the industrial productivity of the nation grew dramatically, especially after the Civil War. America moved into the maturity of an industrial capitalist society by crushing semifeudal patterns in its South, by amassing a giant labor force from the displaced European peasantry and from its own southern and western peasantries, by attracting capital both for venture and for security from the world over, and by spurring productive capacity in a long series of wars.

At the same time, the majority of the people were exploited in a complex process which affected distinct groups differently. Native Americans were driven from their lands in near-genocidal patterns. Slaves were converted first into a rural peasantry of tenant farmers and sharecroppers and then into a secondary labor market for the industries and service sectors of the North. Chicanos were converted into a migrant and stationary agricultural proletariat as well and were partially drawn into the secondary urban labor market with other peoples of color. European and Asian immigrants were lured with the promise of riches to staff the mines and factories and build the railroads of the new industrial base. In turn women of these groups were sought as cheap labor, especially in textiles, where men demanded higher wages. All these peoples and groups of people were whirled together in an exploding and expanding nation. Each was often pitted against the other, not only by conspiracy (although that too) but also, and mainly, by the complexity and dynamism of the new social experience organized around chaotic markets of capital, commodities, and labor.

The story of the nation throughout this period is paradoxically marked by the combination of a single and shallow official history and a pluralism of forgotten and repressed particular histories. On the official side of the myth were the melting pot and the WASP ideal (never real even for most WASPs); on the other were the separate stories of the many racial/ethnic groups and women, whose unique tales—both in their separateness and in their commonality—carry a rich stream of dreams and hopes, as well as of tragedies and bitter struggles.

These separate forces simply could not come together so long as the nation was young, still filling its spaces and expanding outwards. People were structurally running from one another and from themselves rather than discovering at the same time both the self and the other again in uniqueness and commonality. Finally, their separate and common sufferings were consoled and even hidden by the dream of upward mobility and "making it"—a real fact for a significant minority of the working classes, at least so long as expansion continued.

American expansion, however, was not a consistent process; it was marked by severe crises, such as the depression of the 1930s. As a result of periodic crises beginning after the Civil War, a socialist American Left began to emerge. Counting among its ranks such great names as Gene (Eugene V.) Debs, the American Left attempted in varying degrees to challenge the negative elements of American society, while affirming its best promises. The American Left remained weak in contrast to its European counterparts and under the Palmer Raids of the 1920s and the McCarthy purge of the 1950s was subjected to massive repression.

There were many reasons, however, other than repression, for the weakness of the American Left. America was a young and unstable nation. Its working class was racially, culturally, linguistically, regionally, and sexually divided. Finally, at critical points, the system was able to "deliver the goods" for a significant number of workers, in addition to promising generous opportunity for upward mobility in a distinct American climate of egalitarianism.

The third period begins with American defeat in Vietnam and the end of the Cold War, with the recent crisis of both supply and price around raw materials and energy sources like oil, and with the structural inability of the social system to support its population. This is the limit of the American experience, the close-out of the frontier which even President Kennedy could not expand. In one sense it marks the end of all that America has been so far, but in another sense it marks the beginning of a search for an authentically common, but pluralist, identity and purpose. In this latter sense, it is perhaps the true beginning of the history of the *American* people. (The philosopher Hegel argued that American history would not truly begin until this point was reached.) In this latter sense too, it is a period of great creativity but also a period of great danger.

We might speak now of two separate scenarios projected out of this crisis. There is no absolute compulsion that history go either of these two ways, and indeed history is always more cunning than human imagination, but let us project two polar opposites.

The first scenario, and the more probable based on the present course, is for "friendly fascism" in the land. For many reasons the nation is not able to make good on the promises which nourished the personal struggles of so many of America's working-class people. We might foresee a tendency of downward social mobility across all sectors of the population, coupled by higher visibility for the social elite. High rates of unemployment will be taken as normal, as well as decreasing purchasing power for workers. Consumption will go down among the lower and middle classes. In turn, competition over scarce economic resources could intensify, causing bitter tensions along racial, sexual, and ethnic lines, as well as geographic division. This in turn would generate great social unrest, requiring strong repression of the labor movement and of leftist political forces. Force could begin to replace persuasion in the system and government in general could take on a repressive character. There might still be elections, but the realm of choice would be limited. In addition, American capital might be drawn more into lucrative foreign investments, while the domestic economy might be structured around financial and technical management of a global system and the defense production required for it. The American dream would at worst turn into a nightmare, or at best into a sad disappointment.

The second scenario would be some form of "socialist challenge" to the present structures of American society. Given the weak and divided state of the present American Left, it would be difficult to say at this point what shape that might take. The point, however, remains that it would be theoretically possible to undertake a fundamental restructuring of the nation in all its relationships—a restructuring which could improve the quality of life for all, while simultaneously eliminating the structural exploitations of contemporary capitalism.

Given the still weak stage of the American Left and the acceleration of the present structural crisis, the odds for triumph of this second alternative in the short run are very weak. Those interested in fundamental restructuring of American society, therefore, should probably be thinking in long-range terms, although the potential radicalization of American populism should not be ruled out.

Of course present history is so volatile and unstable that future paths of the American nation may not at all correspond to this projected analysis. The projections, therefore, are only tentative and subject to ongoing revision in future reflection.

Author's Note and Acknowledgements

This present essay represents for me personally the first corner in a triangle of work which I hope to be able to complete over the next few years. That triangle is made up of three traditions, distinct but overlapping, which bear on my own present problematic, namely, the American tradition, the Catholic tradition, and the Marxian tradition. This first essay is, of course, only an initial probe into the American tradition. I hope that it can be corrected and deepened by ongoing critical and creative dialogue. The second element in the triangle, the Catholic tradition, is presently occupying my concerns, and I hope that an essay in that area will be forthcoming in the future. The third element—more explicit reflections on the Marxian tradition itself—I have been postponing for later, out of the presumption that it would be more creative to let grapplings with the American and Catholic traditions first take shape and thereby influence the approach to the Marxian tradition. Obviously, however, there is a dialectical relation operating.

In addition, I hope to have the opportunity at some time in the future to grapple with other areas which are often poorly treated (if at all) by the Marxian tradition. Examples would be: (1) the relationship between symbology, spirituality, and social change from a Christian-Marxian perspective; (2) the shifting experience of family life and its potentially creative role in fundamental social change; and (3) potential cooperation between religion and workers' movements in the new world situation. Whether future circumstances will make such grappling possible, I do not know, but these seem critical areas for investigation.

Several words of thanks are called for: first, to Mary Burke and to Bill Ryan, collaborators on the Research Coordination Team for Theology in the Americas and the most consistent critics of this work;

second, to the many people in the Theology in the Americas process who labored through several drafts and offered such rich criticism and insight; third, to Eileen Milby, Eileen Olsen, and Kathy O'Toole, who typed the many drafts and added their own suggestions to the text; and last, to Sergio Torres and Virginia Fabella, who provided vision and perseverance through the entire process of Theology in the Americas. It is my hope that the interpretation of the American Journey in all its cultural, political, and economic complexity will grow deeper still, both critically and creatively, with the ongoing Theology in the Americas search.

Perhaps to these words of thanks should be added an apology to the many scholars who undoubtedly understand parts or the whole of the American Journey far better than I and who, because of my own shortcomings in terms of familiarity with their work, do not find their insights reflected here. The point of this essay, however, is not to offer a finished interpretation of the American experience but simply to whet the taste of all of us for some dimensions that are not part of our ordinary consciousness. For that reason it is not an academic treatise (though such treatises certainly have their place) but a "working document" in an exploratory process. Of course the shortcomings, even in this working document, are my own responsibility and hardly the fault of those who throughout the process have been such warm critics and friends.

It is further to be hoped that the process of criticism and creativity will continue, drawing into it even those who have not been exactly "friends" of the process. It is no secret that some people are angry at what has begun in Theology in the Americas; neither is it a secret that much has already been learned from the assaults of even the severest critics. That may be no consolation to such critics, but the complexity of the American Journey is such that there is no monopoly on insight within any sector.

Finally, it should be made clear that the views expressed here have no official status within the Center of Concern. By encouraging intellectual pluralism, the Center has provided a warm climate of personal support for these explorations, without accepting the Marxian assumptions which tentatively lay behind them. By respecting a diversity of viewpoints and exploring in dialogue alternative views, each opening on an alternative future, the Center has provided a fertile environment for learning and criticism. Such an open milieu has proved creative both in the life of the Center of Concern and also in the broader process which is Theology in the Americas.

Let us now turn to examine in more detail this particular interpretation of the American social struggle in all its complexity.[6]

I. America's Infancy: Independence and Democracy

The American economy on the eve of the Revolution was strong. It was based mainly on agriculture but also shipbuilding. In addition, the colonies were developing their own industrial base, and by 1775 Maryland and Virginia alone had 72 iron foundries. Moreover, the colonies possessed vast natural resources and owned 40% of the British fleet. The agricultural sector, both in the large slave plantations and in the small pioneer farms, made the colonies self-sufficient in food and supplied abundant and profitable exports. Further, the westward expansion, already underway, brought wealth to the upper classes of the coast from land speculation and trade.

The people who made the American economy produce, however, were its workers, namely the black slaves, the white indentured servants—two groups which together comprised an estimated 80% of all immigrants who came to the colonies[1]—small farmers, mechanics, artisans, sailors, dockworkers, and unskilled laborers. The white indentured servants made up perhaps as much as 65% of all white immigrants before 1776. They came fleeing unemployment, religious wars, and extreme poverty. Among them were 50,000 convicts, many of whom had been imprisoned in England for failure to pay small debts. Among them also were countless children and adults who had been kidnapped for sale in America.

Indentured servants, however, constituted a weak labor market, both because their term of bondage was necessarily limited and because they could easily escape into the general population. But captured Africans could be enslaved permanently and kept apart from the general population. Their bondage, too, could be ideologically justified under the "Curse of Ham." With the growth of rice, tobacco, and indigo production on the Southern plantations, black slaves increased to about 500,000 by 1770, approximately 20% of the colonial population.

In earlier colonial history, the relationship between England and its American colonies evolved into a complementary, rather than exploitative, relationship between two components of an empire. In the decades preceding the War of Independence, however, the English economic base shifted from a mercantilist capitalism, which maintained a sense of the common good and corporate responsibility, to a laissez-faire style, which yielded the common good in favor of more aggressive capital accumulation. This shift within England flowed from the ascendancy of industrial capitalism over the earlier mercantilist and agrarian form. The net result externally was that the screws began to be tightened on the colonies.

Life was already harsh for most of the American work force. While the unique hardship of black slaves is well known, the lesser but still severe hardship of white workers is not so often recalled.

> Hours of work were usually from dawn to dusk, and wages for the laborers and sailors were barely enough to support a family.[2]

In the decades preceding the revolution, as the screws were tightened on the American colonies, the burden fell heavily on colonial workers. In 1765, a severe economic depression lasting 20 years settled on the colonies and further pressed down the workers. Unemployment grew, and purchasing power was cut. As a result, the American workers were in no mood to accept further taxation from the British crown. At the same time, colonial workers mingled their resistance to England with resistance to ruling classes here at home. They pressed for democratic political structures as well as liberation from England.

The rich planters and merchants of the colonial aristocracy also objected to the pressures being brought by England. While some of the elite sided with England, particularly those of the middle colonies with financial interests in English trading firms, these Tories lost out to the stronger separationist wing of their class. The time was seen as ripe to make a bid for American independence. The nation was strong and its workers resentful of the mother country. What is generally not recognized, however, is that the upper classes were also and of necessity making a bid for a *separate American empire*.[3]

Managing a mercantilist nation which depended on international trade to unload its surplus and to provide the capital for further expansion, the upper classes could not isolate themselves from the international market without unleashing a radical challenge to domestic social structures. Indeed such challenges were present, albeit in vague form, among American workers, often referred to as the "mob" or "rabble" in the literary testimony of the colonial elite. This mob or rabble proved valuable in thrusting off the British yoke, but challenges to the control of domestic ruling classes could not be tolerated. The forceful suppression of Shays' Rebellion following the Revolution is the most dramatic example of that intent.

The imperialist spirit was widespread among the Northern and Southern upper classes, and the words of Sam Adams typify it well.[4] "An empire is arising in America," he said, as he called for a war of independence and the annexation of Canada, Nova Scotia, and the fishing banks. He also urged further westward expansion and warned of the danger of Catholic infiltration from Canada, where England had just granted religious freedom to Catholics in the Quebec Act. Within two years after Sam Adams' Sons of Liberty tossed the East India Company's tea into Boston Harbor, John Adams stated that it was likely that the seat of the empire would soon be in the American colonies. Sam Adams then called for the Second Continental Congress to write "a constitution to form a great empire." Even Tom Paine pointed out that one third of British trade was carried in American-built ships and that Europe was dependent on American agriculture. William Henry Drayton of South Carolina declared,

> The Almighty. . . has made choice of the present generation to erect The American Empire. . . [It] bids fair, by the blessings of God, to be the most glorious of any upon record. . .[5]

While the independence movement had broad popular support among ordinary "mechanics and farmers" in the nation, the political power of independence was not put in ordinary hands. Enlightenment political theory stressed

> that all men are created equal, that they are endowed by their Creator with certain unalienable rights; that among these are life, liberty, and the pursuit of happiness; . . .[6]

But the reality remained unequal. Native Americans continued to be uprooted by the westward expansion (backed by the land speculations of the East Coast upper classes) and even came under direct genocidal attack. African Americans were still slaves and would continue to be so for a century, thereafter being denied their basic human rights in other ways. The Eastern aristocracy worked to keep political and economic control over the westward movement. The "men" who were created equal were just that, men and not women; women would be granted the right to vote only much later and even at the time of this writing are denied full equality under the Constitution. Freedom and equality were then very much for the wealthy, male, white, and propertied classes.

Yet the controlling classes needed the workers to win victory against the English. Thus, the independence movement was required to accept, in form at least, the democratic movement. But in the revolutionary struggle, two distinct interpretations of democracy came into coalition for the common purpose of fighting the English. One viewed humanity's "inalienable rights" within the framework of individual property, the other within the framework of individual conscience. The language of the Declaration of Independence drafted in 1776 was sufficiently vague to cover both, because the drafters did not yet feel the need to protect themselves against the unpropertied majorities."[7] In the words of Staughton Lynd, underlying these two views were two definitions of freedom:

> ...on the one hand, freedom defined as control over the finished products of human activity; on the other hand, freedom defined as self-determining human activity itself . . . .[8]

The source of the property framework was the conservativeness of the controlling classes; the source of the second was radicalism in the tradition of the Dissenters and the English Levellers' movement. Both drew on the thought of John Locke, but the Dissenters, like Thomas Paine and the English publicists on whom he drew, had radicalized Locke's position.

The latent conflict between the two interpretations, and the distinct social classes which lay behind the separate interpretations, came to a head in the Philadelphia Convention of 1787, which gathered to draw up a constitution for a new nation. Frightened already by the rioting of debt-ridden farmers and mechanics the year before in Massachusetts, the leadership of the propertied aristocracy excluded from its gathering the "radical" revolutionary leaders such as Paine. The design of government which flowed from the secret meetings was at once an acceptance of formal legal democracy and a structured guarantee against the "rabble" having too much influence. In the view of many, the "rights of property" had triumphed over the "rights of man." John Krout acknowledges,

> The Federalists, as the supporters of the proposed Constitution were called, were able to mobilize powerful forces in the struggle over ratification. They enlisted most of the business and financial interests, the professional classes, and the influential newspaper editors. They had money, they were well-organized, and they were led by some of the most prominent men in the country, including Alexander Hamilton, James Madison, and John Jay, authors of *The Federalist*, a collection of essays providing the most cogent analysis and defense of the constitution. . .[9]

The fight over ratification was close and bitter in Massachusetts, Virginia, Pennsylvania, and New York, while North Carolina and Rhode Island had not yet ratified when Washington assumed the presidency in 1789. Thus there was laid in the very foundation of the American nation a prejudice in favor of the "form" of democracy but against its "content." (Critics contrast this "formal democracy" with "substantive democracy," which raises the question of economic rights as well as political rights. What keeps the form from achieving integrity is the structural political advantage given to the classes who control production.)

The young nation was already, therefore, a class-stratified society with political advantage given to the dominating classes—not directly, as in the feudal system, but through the mediation of political structures prejudiced in their favor. "Checks and balances" meant checking popular will (the reckless "rabble"), as well as preventing tyranny, and adding enough structural weight to the minority elite so that it could counterbalance and outmaneuver threatening tendencies from within the popular majority.

In this foundational period, there were also other forces of resistance, in addition to the Northeastern "rabble." These forces may have understood little about structures, but they knew a lot about oppression. Some Native Americans, after patiently enduring great suffering, finally turned to armed resistance to stave off extermination. The slave population, as we know, did not accept its lot meekly. It developed elaborate cultural and political strategies of resistance, culminating in a series of insurrections which constantly kept their masters on the defensive. The small farmers of the westward movement refused to be tamed by Eastern control, leaving even to this day a resentment across the Midwest against the Eastern "establishment." Of the women, we still know too little of their hidden history, but the image of the strong American woman of the frontier, carried on later by a black slave woman such as Sojourner Truth and a white labor woman such as Mary ("Mother") Jones, or colonial women such as Molly Pitcher or Nancy Hart (and the countless other poor women who went with their husbands into battle and bore arms in the Revolution), has left its mark.

The harshness of the class-stratified society was lessened, however (for European Americans at least), by the escape valve of the Western frontier. They could always break out to go it on their own, staking their claim and beginning subsistence farming. Later, industrial expansion would provide a similar escape valve of "upward mobility" for a small stratum of the industrial working class. Together this geographic and industrial space in American society would create a powerful myth of "making it"—the notion that the individual could always break out, get away, and make it alone.

As a result, *freedom* in the foundational period came to be identified with moving out into empty spaces (geographic or economic). This was theoretically reinforced by the liberal philosophical outlook which saw the common good as the net result of so many atomic units doing their own thing. In America, the spaces were there in abundance and they would be nearly two centuries in getting filled. In a certain sense, prior to having reached its limits and turned back in upon itself, America, as Hegel wrote, could not make its own history.[10] Freedom, then, developed as a flight—flight from the corruption of the Old World and flight from other people.

This notion of freedom as flight was aggravated by the sense of religious chosenness in the Puritan foundation. America was a New Israel, redeemed from the sin of Europe. Later, out of this sense of election, would grow the American myth of a New Adam in a nation of innocence.[11] Then it would not be hard for innocence to yield to a savior complex, as "Superman" became the logical descendant of the redeemed Puritan. Here a new beginning untouched by sin (i.e., history) was possible. The sense of election, however, legitimated an arrogant brutality in the foundation, as those who were not part of the righteous were seen as evil, be they natives, poor whites, black slaves, or even Catholics. In a framework of election, all evil is transferred to those outside, and this in turn justifies inflicting atrocities on them.

Of course the nation was made up of much more than redeemed Puritans, even in New England itself. The "rabble" of the Massachusetts colony included former prisoners, prostitutes, beggars, radicals, rogues, and vagabonds.[12] But the power of the Puritan myth over national life testifies to the economic and political hegemony which the upper classes of the Northeast held for so long.

Social resistance too, however, frequently carried religious overtones. Native Americans saw the white intruder violating the covenant with the earth, the source of all religious mystery. Afro-American slaves found in the biblical stories told by white masters the tale of their own oppression. European-American populist churches on the frontier, distant from class or clerical control, developed a true people's religion. The Anabaptist tradition also sought refuge and opportunity on the frontier, giving a millennial character to much American religious language. The more radical view of freedom as human rights rather than property rights had its roots in dissenting English religious movements which proclaimed that the common people could know truth directly, be it religious or political. These religious movements not only supplied alternative myths and a language of resistance; their organizations and buildings also later provided the institutional foundation for a resistance network. For instance, black spirituals provided a secret form of communication, hidden from the white overseer and coding important information on social resistance and escape routes in the Underground Railroad. The later farm-labor movement organized itself on the farm side very much out of white fundamentalist, but people-controlled, churches. And great labor leaders like Gene Debs and Mother Jones would stir peoples' hearts because they talked like preachers. Making a plea for labor unity during the Pullman strike of the 1890s, Debs cried out, "Teach arrogant grinders of the faces of the poor that there still is a God of Israel, and if need be, a Jehovah—a God of battles."[13] And Mother Jones was famous for her Catholic statement, "Pray for the dead, but fight like hell for the living."[14] This continuing tradition perhaps reached unparalleled heights in the dramatic social preaching of Martin Luther King, Jr.

The populist religious instinct of itself, however, provides no social analysis or programmatic structural vision, except in the most general terms. As a result, it faces the danger of remaining unguided beyond immediate struggles, of growing weary in frustration, or even of following socially divisive or co-opted strategies.

Out of the early American religious experience came two important contributions, namely, the separation of church and state and the acceptance of pluralism among religious groups. Even though the origin of these contributions is due more to the inability of any one religious group to dominate than to the absence of that desire, humanity is still richer for the contribution. On the other hand, the separation of church and state and the climate of religious pluralism left economic forces more autonomous from moral questioning and created a climate where value questions were marginalized. As a result, religion increasingly became privatized, and the state (tipped toward the propertied classes) assumed moral authority. Out of this condition flowed a civil religion, the basic instrument of which became the public school system; the basic philosophical orientation, pragmatism.

This, then, is the American foundation. Rather than being monolithic, it contains complex social struggles from the beginning. On the one hand, the controlling classes view property rights as fundamental, and their perspective triumphs in the Federalist position. On the other hand, there is a radical dissenting movement, supported by artisans, small farmers, and laborers, which sees human rights (including economic rights) as fundamental. The first group wins out in the structuring of the central government, but the battle hardly ends there. The structures of formal democracy, weighted against popular will and favoring elite power, prove a dynamic political framework for competing interests among the economically and regionally divided national elite. Against that structure, however, the cry of full democracy, for all people and for all areas of life, continues to be raised. Culturally, the notion of freedom was negative, stressing independence and even flight, with emphasis on property to the right and on conscience to the left. Religiously the Puritan foundation supported the power of the upper classes, while the dissenting movements came more from the popular classes.

In addition to those who clustered around these two interpretations, there were others who still remained outside. Despite the fact that the groups of workers who provoked the British into the Boston Massacre contained a free black by the name of Crispus Attucks (later to be buried in a common martyr's grave with the five other dead workers), most African Americans were still slaves. Likewise, the indigenous peoples of the land, the Indians, were not a party to the discussion over which definition of freedom would triumph. And finally, women were excluded from the political arena, both as voters and officeholders.

The American nation was born, then, neither totally innocent, for injustice shaped it, nor totally evil, for its best promises are still the hope of most of its people. The question of how democracy is interpreted—around property rights or around human rights—remains a living question.

II. America's Adolescence: The Frontier and Expansion

The controlling classes of the young nation were well aware of the tension between the two interpretations of democracy and of the social conflict generated by it. The way they quickly chose to keep alive the sense of promise from the foundation, without yielding their position of power, was simple and really the only structural route available to them. The solution was expansion, across both territorial and industrial frontiers, together with expansion's constant handmaid—war.

Expansion is a fundamental law of capitalism, at least as we have known it so far.[1] Unlike what occurred under feudalism, when the surplus wealth extracted from the labor force was ostentatiously used to reinforce the social superiority of the higher classes, surplus wealth under capitalism is reinvested for further growth. It takes cultural expression in the inner-worldly asceticism (Protestant work ethic) and the sense of predestination from the Calvinist tradition.[2] The continuous growth, however, is periodically interrupted by crisis when markets are saturated and production must be slowed down, causing great social upheaval. In this process the more advanced capitalist elements are able to buy up failing capitalists and to further centralize economic power in the society. It is from this process—the competitive "accumulation of capital" for reinvestment—that our present socio-economic system takes the name *capitalism*.

Expansion naturally creates social upheaval, so that the system appears dynamic as opposed to its more stable and tradition-oriented predecessor, feudalism. The system creates social upheaval externally as it invades new territories, shattering the old economic, political, and cultural structures. It also maintains social upheaval internally by first displacing agrarian workers from the land as a result of the introduction of capitalist techniques into traditional agricultures and then turning the former peasantry into an industrial proletariat. This is the root of the urbanization phenomenon from Elizabethan England to the United States ghettoes to the sprawling slums of the Third World. The urban migration, however, is itself subsequently disrupted as many urban industrial workers are rendered superfluous by automation, a capital-intensive process accelerated by the competition of the market place. Automation and, subsequently, cybernation displace large sectors of the work force and create massive unemployment. Unemployment is further aggravated as capitalists are forced by the structure of competition to search for the cheapest labor markets, at first creating only regional manipulation of labor markets within countries but eventually issuing in global manipulation of labor markets under multinational corporations.

In this process, no capitalist enterprise can include in its accounting the true social and ecological costs of production, for the resulting higher price of its products would be underbid in the market by those enterprises which do not calculate such costs. Thus the capitalist enterprise, although it incredibly increases humanity's technical development and productive capacity, creates a structural system characterized by social and ecological recklessness. This can be tamed sometimes by political reform, but that reform is generally undercut in new ways by fresh strategies which either maneuver around its law or intervene from outside territorial limits.

The constant recklessness of the system's basic structures (unable really to care for all people or for nature) generates what some have referred to as a structural violence, hidden in class warfare and marketplace competition, but obvious in the great wars waged for control of natural resources and market outlets for surplus production. Even the socialist nations, when they enter the international market, operate more or less under structural laws of capitalism.

The social upheaval of capitalism was strong in the young American nation. The two faces of expansion—external geographical outreach and internal growth in productive capacity—rose upon two separate but related pillars of injustice, namely, imperialism abroad and exploitation of the labor force at home. Let us first examine the territorial expansion of the system.

Territorial Expansion: Speculators, Pioneers, Natives, Latins, and the Third World

At the end of the 18th century, the United States of America extended west only as far as the Mississippi River and did not reach south to touch the Gulf of Mexico. By the middle of the 19th Century, it reached the Pacific Coast and its present southern boundaries. About half of that territory was acquired by purchases from the old European colonial powers (England, France, and Spain); the other half was acquired by war.

The westward movement was greatly accelerated by the economic crisis of 1837, when many people, ruined by inflation, simply moved on. The central section of the United States was bought from France in 1803 as the Louisiana Purchase, and the southeastern gulf coast was purchased from Spain in the first two decades of the 19th century. That left three territories to be won, namely, Texas, Oregon, and California.

American trappers in British Oregon began a war of nerves with British trappers of the Hudson Bay Company. After the virtual extermination of fur-bearing animals in that area, Britain agreed to a territorial compromise in 1846, ceding the Oregon Claim to the United States. Assaults were already underway on the Mexican territories of California and Texas. Mexico went to war in defense of its territory but lost, ceding its rights in the Treaty of Guadalupe Hidalgo (1848), which fixed the Rio Grande as the southwest boundary of the United States.

The expansionist fever was part of the growing nationalist sentiment known as "Manifest Destiny." Daniel S. Dickinson of New York gave it the following formulation before the Senate in 1848:

> But the tide of emigration and the course of empire have since been westward. Cities and towns have sprung up on the shores of the Pacific. . . . Nor have we yet fulfilled the destiny allotted to us. New territory is spread out for us to subdue and fertilize; new races are presented for us to civilize, educate and absorb; new triumphs for us to achieve for the cause of freedom. North America presents to the eye one great geographical system. . . it is soon to become the commercial center of the world.[3]

The real victims of this expansionist movement, however, were not Mexico or the European powers but the Indian and northern Mexican peoples who communally farmed the lands seized in the annexations. The native Indians were moved on, or destroyed, while the northern Mexicans (also heavily Indian) were converted into a rural agricultural proletariat. The natives and the northern Mexicans were the first peoples to come face to face with the young but growing empire.

Tomás Almaguer notes six stages of American expansion between 1803 and 1853, concluding with the seizure of the vast northern Mexican territories, and increasing US territory ten times in half a century. According to Almaguer,

> These North American aggressions on Mexico must be understood in the context of the rise and expansion of American capitalism. . . the development and expansion of industrial capital necessitated the expansion and conquest of new territories.[4]

The newly conquered Indio-mestizo Mexican population then became an internal colony available as a super-exploitable labor force, integral to the development of Western agriculture, of the early mining and railroad industries, and finally of the broader industrial-reserve army in which it would serve a part.

A similar and perhaps even more tragic fate awaited Native American tribes in this expansion process. The first European settlers of the Northeast had been welcomed by the natives and probably would not have endured without their aid. The natives gave them food and taught them to survive. Later, Chief Red Jacket of the Senecas would remind the young nation,

We first knew you, a feeble plant, which wanted a little earth whereon to grow. We gave it to you; and afterward, when we could have trod you under our feet, we watered and protected you. . . . When you first came here, you clung around our knee and called us fathers; we took you by the hand and called you brothers.[5]

As expansion tried to crush the native, Tantanka Yotanka (Sitting Bull), soon to be assassinated at Standing Rock, would remark how the European civilization oppressed not only his people, but all poor people:

These people have many rules that the rich may break, but the poor must keep. They take tithes from the poor and weak to support the rich who rule.[6]

The native resistance was finally crushed, militarily if not spiritually, and the heirs of those who had cared for the first Europeans would lament through the voice of Chief Joseph,

It is cold and we have no blankets. The little children are freezing to death. My people, some of them have run away to the hills and have no blankets, no food; no one knows where they are—perhaps freezing to death. I want to have time to look for my children and see how many I can find. Maybe I shall find them among the dead.[7]

The conflict between the invading Euro-American civilization and the native and mestizo peoples, like the conflict with the African Americans and indeed with all colonial areas, was certainly an economic conflict. Robert Allen notes,

Indeed, it is no exaggeration to suggest that the Industrial Revolution, which enabled Europe and North America to leap far ahead of the rest of the world in material welfare, would have been delayed by several centuries if not for the capital yielded by colonialism.[8]

Moreover, the resulting social structure which followed from the internal and external colonial programs of capitalism strongly followed racial lines. Commenting on the organization of production in the United States, Robert Blauner observes,

From the very beginning race has been central to the social relations of production in America. The right to own property, the right not to become property, and the distribution of labor were all essentially matters of color. Southern slavery was a system of production based on race. But not only in the ante-bellum South, elsewhere and after, the racial principle continued to organize the structure of the labor force and the distribution of property. The free laborers, the factory proletariat, was largely recruited from white ethnic groups, whereas people of color (Mexicans, Asians, to a lesser degree Indians, and, of course, blacks) were employed in various unfree labor situations. The ethnic labor principle appears to be a universal element of the colonial situation and this is why race and racism are not simply aspects of cultural "superstructure," but cut through the entire social structure. . . .[9]

Until the Second World War, peoples of color in the United States were generally confined to pre-capitalist sectors of the American economy. With the war and after, as the pre-capitalist sectors were invaded by capitalist styles of organization, the peoples of color began to be shifted to an urban, capitalist base, although of course to the lowest rungs on the ladder. But this story belongs to later discussion.

The conflict was not simply economic, however, because it is perhaps the cultural heritage of the colonized peoples, as well as their color, which accounted for the caste-like social structuring. The vision and values required by the capitalist mode of production—values which grew out of the dominating strands of white, Western civilization—were generally foreign to these peoples. It was easier to gather the peasantries and proletariat of white Europe into the new social structures and to train them in the new values (although even these groups still retain strong cultural defenses, such as family and neighborhood, against total cultural penetration) than to do so for the peoples of color. For this reason, the peoples of color were called backward, but really they were preserving a fundamentally different vision of how people should live together, of humanity's relation with nature, and even of the religious mystery. These peoples, whose cultural roots in communal or tribal societies were still strong, would not so easily be drawn into a fragmented world based on social and ecological exploitation. This was especially true in the case of Native Americans, and the words of an old holy Wintu woman tell it well:

> How can the spirit of the earth like the white man? . . . everywhere the white man has touched it, it is sore.[10]

Neither innocent nor fully blameworthy in this story are the pioneers. It was they—poor and struggling families—who were pitched into conflict with the native peoples. Their story is similar to that of the contemporary white working class—neither the instigators nor the worst victims of policies which trap them in between. The westward movement was deliberately planned by American economic elites, partly for the financial gain from land speculation and partly as a requirement of early American capitalism, which sought to avoid monarchy to the right and class war to the left.[11] Constant expansion kept the social system in a regular state of imbalance, blocking the accumulation of power in a single figure but also keeping the populace itself disunited. This quite conscious policy was worked out early on by men like Jefferson, Monroe, and Franklin (a major land speculator). Jefferson, in fact, was quite willing to sacrifice the native population and aggressively encouraged policies that led in that direction in order to guarantee a favorable environment. Washington, however, had been more cautious and taken a long-range view of the development of the empire. He tried to develop the West slowly, hoping to assure stability and a reasonable arrangement with the native peoples. But he was unsuccessful.

Beginning early on with the settling of Kentucky and climaxing later with the Free Soil movement, the economic elites sustained a policy of reckless expansion, one which provided no plan and no care for those who were being brutally injured in the process. Into this vacuum rushed the endless number of poor settlers, seeking desperately to escape from indentured-servant status or from bitter poverty. They came out of Europe, many of them also displaced as peasantries by the forces of burgeoning capitalism, which could not care for its people there and was only too happy to be rid of them. They came to a young America, the economic elites of which did not care for them either but were willing to use their bodies and lives to push forward the expansionist scheme. In the absence of human social planning, and under the guidance only of profit maximization and territorial control, the situation forced red and white poor peoples into a deadly battle against each other.

Once the Pacific was reached, a base had been established for expansion beyond the nation's shores. Almaguer, in part quoting LaFeber notes:

> Once continental expansion was complete, American capitalists shifted their search for new markets and sources of raw materials on to overseas areas. American overseas investment began spiraling and "by the 1870's the staggering rise in exports changed the historically unfavorable balance of American trade to a favorable balance which would last at least through the first half of the twentieth century. . . By 1893, American trade exceeded that of every country in the world except England." By this time the United States had already asserted itself as a principal participant in the world capitalist market, and the groundwork had been laid for becoming the undisputed leader of the world imperialist system at the end of World War II.[12]

American expansion was soon on its way to the Third World.[13] The Monroe Doctrine (1823) and its subsequent redefinitions laid the US commercial and military claim to Latin America, while in 1853 Commodore Perry was opening contacts with Japan. By 1889, the US Navy, which Jefferson had argued would be the military foundation of the empire, routed the Spanish across the New World. With its victory, the United States seized the Philippines, Guam, and Puerto Rico, as well as economic and political control of Cuba. Secretary of State John Hay's "Open Door" policy (1889) laid US capital's bid for China and was followed up by the landing of US Marines to quell the so-called Boxer Rebellion. In 1867 the US Navy seized the Midway Islands, a thousand miles west of Hawaii. In 1899, Hawaii was forcefully annexed. Soon the United States was dividing the Samoan Islands with Germany. By 1910, American bankers were heavily financing railroads in China, while cheap Chinese labor was flowing back to the United States. The Panama Canal, carved out of Colombian territory, linked the Atlantic and Pacific outreach.

Within a century, therefore, US interests had spanned the continent, reached out to both Latin America and the Orient, and linked two oceans. Until Franklin D. Roosevelt replaced the "Big Brother" policy with the "Good Neighbor" policy, the United States had militarily intervened upon Latin American sovereignty 14 times. (In more recent days, through overt and covert intervention in Guatemala, the Dominican Republic, Chile, Vietnam, Cambodia, and Laos, those outreaches have been continued.) Japanese and American imperialist rivalries in the Pacific grew aggravated, until they climaxed in Pearl Harbor. Africa had been plundered early on for slaves (while in our time the white apartheid regimes of South Africa and the now-collapsed Portuguese colonies received strong US backing). The only areas remaining for penetration were Europe and Canada, both to become major areas of US economic domination in the post-World War II era.

Perhaps the crassest expression of this imperialism came from Senator Albert J. Beveridge, when he announced,

> We will not renounce our part in the mission of our race, trustees under God, of the civilization of the world. God has not been preparing the English-speaking and Teutonic peoples for a thousand years for nothing but vain and idle self-contemplation and self-admiration. No! He has made us the master organizers of the world adept in government that we may administer government among savages and senile peoples.[14]

Only a tiny minority, however, of the English-speaking Teutonic peoples were really the masters.

It would not be possible in this short space to trace the influence of the evolving economic base and its directing social classes over this expansionist mentality. The laissez-faire capitalism, which had early on triumphed over the mercantilism of the revolution, gave way to *corporate capitalism,* which placed great stress on foreign policy. In the words of William Appleman Williams, the corporate economy

> emphasized increasingly the role of foreign policy in solving domestic troubles and consciously initiated a broad program of sophisticated imperialism. . . . Underlying that expansion, and sustaining it into the twentieth century, was the central idea that overseas expansion provided the *sine qua non* of domestic prosperity and social peace.[15]

By the turn of the century, the United States had become the leading industrial nation of the world. Great Britain, its closest rival, was manufacturing only half as much as the United States. As production grew, so did centralization, and the merger of bank capital and industrial capital followed. So colossal was the wealth being gathered that it became necessary to invest in colonial areas. The whole world soon became the scene of American capital investment, backed up by American military might. The earlier war with Spain had tested American power, and soon it was ready for the European battlefield.

Many American voices resisted imperialism. Republican Senator George Frisbie Hoar of Massachusetts formed the 500,000-member Anti-Imperialist League, and Mark Twain mocked the imperialist rhetoric. The voice of Gene Debs was loud and clear:

> There are thousands who are not swept from their feet by the war craze. They realize that war is national murder, that the poor furnish the victims and that whatever the outcome may be, the effect is always upon the toiling class.[16]

Early socialists and most trade unionists were against war, but national chauvinism was not hard to stir up. Preparing for the war with Spain, bands played, "It'll be a Hot Time in the Old Town Tonight," providing many people in a complex and insecure nation with a sense of national unity and purpose. (This grounding of national identity in a war consciousness continued strong throughout the present century and only came into crisis with Vietnam.)

Territorial expansion came to be paralleled by stepped-up exploitation at home as a result of industrial expansion. These two coincided as linked structural expressions, so that at the very moment that US commercial interests were taking over the old Spanish Empire, lynch-enforced white supremacy was raging in the South, and a near war was underway against the mainly white labor movement in the North. At the same time, severe political pressures were being put on small family farmers. Likewise American women from the middle classes and from the working classes were having their roles dramatically redefined.

Industrial Expansion: Industrialists, Black Slaves, Immigrant White Workers, Farmers, and Women

As early as the time of George Washington, economic questions had been raised about the institution of slavery. It was Washington's feeling, as well as that of many other members of the Southern gentry, that slavery was too costly and inefficient to be of service in an expanding empire. They believed that rather there was needed a larger, cheaper labor force, possessing more skills and independent initiative than a subject slave population. In contrast to many in the Abolitionist movement who tended to see slavery as a moral issue, the architects of the young empire saw it as a structural weakness. It was for this reason, therefore, that a progressive wing of the upper classes supported the elimination of slavery and sought to ban it from the westward movement. It was for this same reason (efficiency) that millions of immigrants were recruited from Europe to form the white working class. There was needed an industrial working class to work the machines of the new industry.

Northern industrialists supported the destruction of the Southern economy and its slave system, because that gave them full political and economic room to build up the capitalist giant emerging in the North.

Prior to the Civil War, Southern agricultural interests were the dominant force in US politics, even financing political campaigns as far north as Boston. The Civil War ended that and put industrial and finance capital in the dominant position.

The experience of the Civil War provides a good example of the shifting class alliances in the political arena within such a complex and unevenly developed nation.[17]

The Northern industrial capitalists were anxious to accelerate industrial capitalism in the South, because its semi-feudal plantation economy left the nation with two separate economies, holding back the development of the whole and weakening America's competitive power in the international market.

Prior to the Civil War, strong political fighting continued between the Northern and Southern upper classes over control of the West. The admission or exclusion of slavery from the new states was the fundamental issue, although earlier Southerners like Washington and Jefferson had tried to exclude slavery from the westward movement.

The struggle peaked with the Civil War, which might be called the Second American Revolution. Just as the first revolution had enlisted the colonial workers in a temporary coalition with the colonial merchants and planters against the English, now the Northern industrialists enlisted Northern workers, the middle classes, and the slaves themselves against the Southern planters. This second revolution became most radical when the industrialists were forced to arm the black population and enlist them in the struggle. Out of this grew a dramatic black movement during the period of Reconstruction which threatened massive land reform across the South; temporarily built alliances with small white farmers of the South and with the Southern white middle class (both of whom formerly bore the tax burden for the plantation owners); created popular assemblies and interracial governments; and defended it all with armed black militia. All of this occurred with the approval of the Northern industrialists, who were anxious to break the political and economic power of the Southern feudal gentry.

So long as the industrialists held their power with strength in the North, they could afford to unleash a democratic revolution in the South. Once other forms of resistance against the industrialists grew, however, they had to betray the black freedom movement in the South and allow the Southern elite to preside over a counterrevolution in the South. The counterrevolution restored near slavery under a tenant-farmer and sharecropper system, backed up by the Black Codes and guerrilla terrorism of the Ku Klux Klan (KKK). Thousands of blacks, who only a few years before had moved to dramatic gains in education, civil rights, and political participation, now became the victims of vicious and murderous attacks encouraged by the elite. Once the Southern gentry knew that federal troops would not back up the

Reconstruction movement, they were free to unleash their reign
of terror.

This assurance came in what is known as the Betrayal of 1877. The
South was in the midst of its brutal battle over the nature of
Reconstruction and, in the opinion of some, even on the verge of another
war. The Republican Party of the Northern industrialists, under attack
in the North from labor and in the West from farmers, was threatened
with losing power. It turned to the Southern planters for an ally.

> After extended dickering, an electoral commission was finally
> established which gave Hayes the contested states of Florida,
> Louisiana, South Carolina and also Oregon, after a crisis which
> lasted three months. An agreement had been reached behind the
> scenes, while the electoral vote was being counted. Through
> intermediaries, Hayes assured the Southern Democrats that in
> return for the Presidency he would grant them complete control of
> South Carolina and Louisiana. The Republican Party bought its
> victory at the price of completely abandoning the Negro masses to
> the tender mercy of counterrevolution.[18]

As a result, the Southern ruling class was able to mount an effective
campaign of splitting the poor whites, small white farmers, and the
Southern middle class from alliance with the black freedom movement.
The wedge was driven between them partly by a campaign of terror
carried out by the KKK and similar groups, partly by an intensive press
campaign exposing corruption among the Republicans (especially
around railroad subsidies), and partly by appealing to white superiority.

The class complexity of the racial issue emerged in this process.
Both freed black laborers and unionized white workers were coming
under simultaneous attacks, but from different sectors. The blacks were
under attack from the old Southern gentry and found their only
establishment ally in the Northern Republican industrialists. Despite
serious efforts to create a national united front by the heavily white
Northern union movement and the black freedom movement coming out
of the South, the political alliances broke down. Southern blacks could
not abandon the Northern Republicans or their cause would certainly be
lost, while the Northern white workers were trying to organize in
opposition to the Republican industrialists. The inability to rise above
this dilemma points to the structural weakness of any political movement
which does raise the most basic class questions. To this day, the question
of the relation of black labor and white labor remains one of the most
fundamental questions in American society. Marx pointed this out in
1867 in his first volume of *Capital*:

> In the United States of America, any sort of independent labor
> movement was paralyzed so long as slavery disfigured a part of the
> republic. Labor with a white skin cannot emancipate itself where
> labor with a black skin is branded.[19]

Despite the destruction of slavery, the problem remained with the semi-feudal system of tenancy and sharecropping which stumbled out of the broken Reconstruction era. It continued later with the displacement of Southern black and white peasants into the industrial areas of the North, where they served and continue to serve as a secondary labor pool, to be hired and fired loosely and kept available for the more menial tasks.

Yet even though a revolutionary coalition between black and white labor did not emerge from the postwar era, it would be a mistake to say strong forces were not working toward the goal. Socialist German workers from the North played a major role in the Abolitionist movement. In New York City on September 13, 1871, when 20,000 workers marched in the eight-hour parade called by the Workingmen's Union, black workers were greeted with resounding applause as they reached the reviewing stands at City Hall. In the words of James Allen,

> This was a great advance. Only a few years before race riots had taken place on the docks when the employers attempted to break a strike of Irish longshoremen by importing Negro dock workers from the border cities.
>
> Similarly after, on December 18, 1871, a company of Negro militia, the Skidmore Guard, participated in a demonstration called by the Internationals to protest the execution of three leading Parisian Communards. A similar demonstration had been broken up the week before by the police. Over 10,000 of all colors and nationalities were in the line of march.[20]

William Sylvis, one of the great names of American labor, devoted his life and energy to the principle of white-black labor solidarity, as well as to the solidarity of working-class men and women.[21] Born of a poverty-stricken Pennsylvania family and never able to raise his own family out of deep poverty, Sylvis was no middle-class liberal. But he knew that freed blacks, formerly locked out of Northern industry, were being hired at reduced wages at the same time that Northern ports were bringing in thousands of industrial indentured servants. Together these groups were being played off against the old Northern labor force and, eventually, against one another.

He knew, too, that women were being pitched into the manipulation, often working from six in the morning until midnight for $3 a week. He found cases of women and children fainting beside their looms and living in horrid urban slums. While the prices of food doubled and even quadrupled, he thought of his own poor children and wife.

Labor leaders in the North were aware that Southern planters, intent on saving their system by replacing slavery with peonage through debt and vagrancy laws, had instigated mass killings of blacks. While 5,000 iron molders were locked out of their plants in Pittsburgh, their leaders in jail dying of starvation, 45 blacks were slain in New Orleans and 46 more taken from their homes and lynched in Pittsburgh.

Well aware of the growing power of finance capital, Sylvis wrote,

> If we can succeed in convincing these people [black workers] to make common cause with us . . . we will have a power . . . that will shake Wall Street out of its boots.[22]

While many trade unionists wanted to reject black offers of cooperation, Sylvis insisted,

> The line of demarcation is between the robbers and the robbed, no matter whether the wronged be the friendless widow, the skilled white mechanic, or the ignorant black. Capital is no respecter of persons and it is in the very nature of things a sheer impossibility to degrade one class of labor without degrading all.[23]

Making the same point about President Andrew Johnson's effort to restore the power of the Southern planters while breaking the black movement, the Boston *Daily Evening Voice* wrote,

> Capital knows no difference between white and black laborers; and labor cannot make any, without undermining its own platform and tearing down the walls of its defense. The whole united power is necessary to the successful resistance of the united power of capital.[24]

The concern for black-white labor solidarity was felt equally from the black side, as told by Isaac Meyers, an outstanding black labor leader of the period, to the 1869 Congress of the National Labor Union. The Congress had passed a resolution the preceding year rejoicing in the abolition of slavery and inviting the "working classes of the South" to join the labor movement. Said Meyers,

> Silent, but powerful and far-reaching is the revolution inaugurated by your act in taking the colored laborer by the hand and telling him that his interest is common with yours. . . . Slavery, or slave labor, the main cause of the degradation of white labor, is no more. And it is the proud boast of my life that the slave himself had a share in striking off the one end of the fetters that bound him by the ankle, and the other end that bound you by the neck.[25]

As a result of frank discussions, the Congress resolved that

> the National Labor Union knows no North, no South, no East, no West, neither color nor sex on the question of the rights of labor.[26]

Definite steps were taken toward the organization of black labor, and a committee was appointed to assist black workers in their organizing efforts in Pennsylvania.

Thus, a movement toward black-white solidarity arose very early in the labor movement. William Sylvis also campaigned for *women's* rights in the labor movement, urging their admission into the National Labor Union. The dominant attitude, however, was rejection. Richard Boyer and Herbert Morais tell the story:

> Most men and most trade unions regarded women workers, whose numbers had mightily increased during the Civil War, as a menace

who drove wages down by taking underpaid jobs when they should have remained at home.

Virtually every trade union refused to admit them, despite the fact that they had been pioneers in the labor movement, inaugurating the trade union press. . . . They had, moreover, conducted some of the earliest mass strikes in American history.[27]

The secret weapon in many strikes was, in fact, the courage and dedication of the women involved.

Perhaps one of the greatest figures in all labor history was a woman by the name of Mary Jones, affectionately known as "Mother" Jones.[28] An Irish immigrant school teacher and later seamstress, Mother Jones became one of the principal organizers of the United Mine Workers of America. When police attacked the miners' pickets and forced them to flee, Mother Jones would round up women who would drive the police away with sticks and brooms, and the strike was on again. Fighting hard for worker solidarity, against the narrow vision of organizing by crafts, she supported the One Big Union concept and was in a prominent position for the opening convention (1905) of the Industrial Workers of the World (IWW), known more often as the "Wobblies." She later supported the Mexican Revolution and went to Mexico subsequently as a "guest of State." A fervent Catholic, she insisted that God Almighty had taught her ". . . to pray for the dead but fight like hell for the living." In 1921, at the Pan-American Labor Federation in Mexico, she supported the Russian Revolution and, despite the opposition of Samuel Gompers, secured adoption of a resolution demanding the release of political prisoners. Fighting for all workers, even going to jail in her eighties, Mother Jones was an American legend. Emma Langdon wrote of her in a 1904 account of the Cripple Creek strike and massacre,

"Mother" is the workers' refuge and inspiration. "Mother" is the cry when overawed by corporate hirelings and scabs they join hands in a common struggle, and "Mother" again when the troops reinforced by hunger are beating them to death.[29]

The original vision of the labor movement was radical, as the intense and prolonged wars between the National Association of Manufacturers and workers' organizations show. There is buried in American history one of the most violent and brutal labor stories in the history of industrialism. To this day, workers around the world rally on May 1 to commemorate the leaders of the Chicago Haymarket demonstration (demanding the eight-hour day), who were later executed by the State of Illinois.

The alliances which defy the contemporary imagination were symbolized by one of those executed, Albert Parsons, a veteran of the Confederate Army, descendant on his father's side of a revolutionary Puritan divine who led his congregation to Bunker Hill, husband of a Mexican-Indian woman by the name of Lucy Gonzales, a fervent reader of Marx, a leader of the Chicago Labor movement and of the

International Working People's Association, and a warm favorite of the foreign-born workers of Chicago.

When the industrialists had Parsons safe in jail, his wife Lucy took up the struggle. Penniless and alone, she dragged her two children across the country speaking day and night to organizations which fought for the innocence of the Haymarket victims. Often insulted and even jailed with her children, she became a major protest movement in her own person. Forbidden to see his beloved wife, Parsons wrote her shortly before his hanging,

> My poor, dear wife . . . You, I bequeath to the people, a woman of people. I have one request to make of you: Commit no rash act when I am gone, but take up the great cause of socialism where I am compelled to lay it down.[30]

The largest early labor organization was Terence V. Powderly's Knights of Labor. Membership in the order grew from 28,000 in 1880 to 100,000 in 1885 to 700,000 in 1886. Sixty thousand blacks joined the order. The foreign-born and unskilled rushed in. Women workers were increasingly active in its ranks, under the direction of Leonora Barry. The slogan of the movement was "An injury to one is an injury to all." Powderly himself was a pacific person, even dissuading strikes. But the hostility and violence which his members encountered at the direction of the National Association of Manufacturers (which employed countless spies and private armies organized by the Pinkerton Company) prompted him at one point to urge,

> I am anxious that each lodge should be provided with powder, shot and Winchester rifles when we intend to strike.[31]

A small early labor organization destined to outlive the Knights of Labor was the Federation of Organized Trades and Labor Unions of the United States and Canada. It had its base among skilled workers organized along craft lines. It was originally very militant. Founded in 1881, it adopted the following preamble to its constitution:

> A struggle is going on in the nations of the world between the oppressors and oppressed of all countries, a struggle between capital and labor which must grow in intensity from year to year and work disastrous results to the toiling millions of all nations if not combined for mutual protection and benefit.[32]

Accepting class struggle, international solidarity, and the strike weapon, the organization made its great issue the eight-hour day.

In the ensuing battle, centered in Chicago, the upper class mustered all its strength in defense. Their feelings were expressed in the *Chicago Tribune* of November 23, 1875, in a comment on a meeting of 50 unemployed persons protesting welfare policies:

> Every lamp-post in Chicago will be decorated with a communist carcass if necessary . . .[33]

"A communist carcass for every lamp-post" soon became a favorite refrain of the *Tribune* in its battle against the eight-hour day.

The political and legal system was strongly prejudiced against the labor movement. Even the Knights of Labor had to begin as a secret organization. After the Civil War in the South, the military command took steps to smash workers' strikes. Military Order No. 65 prohibited the organization of labor unions and picketing and guaranteed military protection to factories employing strikebreakers. A bill introduced into the New York legislature in 1864 termed all labor-union members "criminals" and subjected them to fine and imprisonment. A similar bill was nearly passed in Massachusetts, while the collusion of government and capitalists in Pennsylvania broke the Miner's Association in the eastern coal fields. The struggle to gain simply the right to organize and its indispensable handmaid, the right to strike, was no easy battle (and these rights may still not be secure in the American nation). Force, both legal and illegal, was consistently used against American workers.

At the same time, black lynching grew in the South, and the screws were tightened on white workers in the North. Soon a nationwide railroad strike broke out, and there were bloody battles in Chicago, Pittsburgh, and Baltimore. Women were in the front lines battling with federal troops. In Pittsburgh, the militia refused to obey federal orders and joined the workers instead. The advice of national power broker Tom Scott, who had done much to provoke the violence, was to give the strikers a "rifle diet for a few days."[34] Like the Black Freedom movement, the young and vigorous union movement was temporarily broken.

Several structural factors combined in this process, among them depression and subsequent economic expansion overseas. Another important factor, however, was the combination of racial, ethnic, and sexual divisions within America's giant and heterogeneous labor force.

In the expansion process, more workers were needed. And so recruiters looked abroad. Labor shortage became the reason why most of the 30 million or so European immigrants came to this country from the middle of the last century to the middle of this one. The resulting racial and ethnic division would prove a powerful force in keeping labor divided.

According to the independent journalist John Swinton, writing in 1883 of the tactics in the Pennsylvania coal fields,

The contractors make their appearance under the American flag among the half-starved mudsills in some of the most wretched districts of Hungary, Italy or Denmark, tell the stories of fabulous wages to be gotten in America, bamboozle the poor creatures, rope them in and make contracts with them to pay their passage across the sea, upon their agreeing to terms that few can understand. When they reach the districts of this country to which the contractors ship them, they find their golden dreams turned into nightmares, as they are put to work in mines, factories, or on railroads, at even lower wages than those of them whom they throw out of work . . .[35]

Again in 1884, Swinton wrote that the coal operators were

Pitting the English against the Irish, and vice versa, and the German against both . . . keeping up a constant war of the races.[36]

During the Hocking Valley strike of Ohio coal miners, poor Italian laborers were supplied by a New York concern at 50¢ a day. Swinton wrote of these:

They are hired out and put to work in ignorance of their rights. . . Honest-hearted, hard-working men, . . . these poor fellows from impoverished Italy would not play the part of blacklegs [strikebreakers] if they could help it.[37]

But, wrote Boyer and Morais,

They could not help it. Accordingly, they were frequently herded from steerage to a scene of nightmare violence where they passed between the lines of struggling men, throwing stones and curses into the gates of a struck mill or mine, while riot raged outside. The vicious snap of rifle fire was almost the first sound heard in America by many a bewildered immigrant.[38]

The trade-union movement consistently fought for national legislation to abolish contract labor imported from abroad. A law was finally passed, but there was no effective enforcement machinery. In the fight against such manipulation of labor markets, it was perhaps inevitable that an anti-foreign spirit would arise. The natural response was to want to cut off the foreign labor supply rather than to get to the root of the problem structurally, that is, to the very nature of a system which treats labor as a market commodity. (This question is still not settled, as illustrated by the current debate over "illegals" or "undocumented workers.")

At the same time, struggle—even to the point of arms—was raging in the farm lands where *small farmers* battled the railroads which were evicting them left and right from their lands. Thousands of small farmers organized the powerful Farmers' Alliances, which tried to form a third party for the overthrow of Wall Street domination. In the East, meanwhile, the corporations were busy forming huge monopolies known as trusts and combining into price-fixing pools and wage-fixing pools.

Politically, the separate forces of resistance were never able to achieve strong national unity. The Socialist Party of America, which ran Gene Debs for the presidency, was the strongest single force, but it peaked about 1912 and collapsed after the First World War. The farm-labor movement thereafter continued much of its struggle.

The political question became more complicated as different responses emerged in the American Left to the direction of Russian society. Most American socialists had generally supported the Russian Revolution and saw it as a breakthrough in the social struggle. The split came on the advisability of the Bolshevik party model for the American situation. Some believed it was a peculiar requirement of the struggle against czarist dictatorship and that, left to its own inertia, it was creating totalitarian structures within Russian society. For many, Stalin eventually came to epitomize these fears. Others, however, believed that because the controlling classes would, if really threatened, unleash every weapon in defense of their power (the turn of liberal societies to fascism), only a tightly disciplined political unit could stand up to the threat within the American Left. This remains a complex and unfinished debate.

In the history of American socialism, leadership on the Left belonged for the first two decades of the 20th century to the forces linked to the looser Socialist Party of America.[39] Thereafter, the party declined, rising later only as a party of intellectuals with no mass organization. By the time of the 1930s, leftist leadership had passed to the young Communist Party of America. Organizers from its ranks would become a major force in organizing the Congress of Industrial Organizations (CIO). Their great strength in the movement, however, did not extend to the creation of a socialist vision within the working class. Workers followed the Communist Party organizers as trade-union leaders, but the vision of socialism did not take hold. In fact, the Communist Party played down the question of an alternative vision and stressed "immediate issues" instead.[40]

By the time of climax of the expansion period, however, the question was becoming academic. Both the Socialist Party and the Communist Party receded into marginal positions in the post-World War II era.

Both sexism and racism were central issues within the American Left. The Socialist Party drew a wide range of women, from old American middle-class Protestant backgrounds (coming heavily from church social movements), from the trade-union and farm movements, and from the immigrant working classes of Eastern industrial centers. These included famous names like Ella Reeve Bloor, Anna Luise Strong, Lena Morrow Lewis, Rheta Childe Door, Florence Kelly, Mother Jones, Kate Richards O'Hare, Margaret Sanger, and Rose Pastor Stokes. Not all socialists, however, favored women's suffrage. Some were afraid that the Catholic women's vote would in fact be used against the socialist movement.

The Socialist Party had a spectrum of positions on black participation. Those further to the right, and closer to Progressive politics (which were strongly racist) and to the American Federation of Labor (AFL) leader Samuel Gompers, were nervous about it. Gompers had castigated blacks for letting themselves be used as strikebreakers, warning that the "colored man . . . was tearing down what the white man has built up" (the trade-union movement). Yet he did not lead the AFL into an aggressive program of organization among blacks and allowed the organization openly to violate its constitutional principle of racial equality. Gompers was particularly racist in his anti-Oriental sentiments and even authored a number of anti-Chinese and anti-Japanese pamphlets. Some right-wing and centrist socialists took up openly racist positions. Victor Berger, for instance, warned that socialism could be successful only if the United States was kept a "white man's" country. Those to the left, however, like Bill Haywood and Gene Debs, were militant in their support of black inclusion. Several locals were strongly mixed and the Tennessee platform of 1912 declared that

> ... "the question of race superiority" had been "injected into the mind of the white wage-worker" only as a "tactical method" of the "capitalist class" to keep the workers divided on the economic field.[41]

Some socialists were involved in the founding of the National Association for the Advancement of Colored People (NAACP), and W.E.B. DuBois was for a time a Socialist Party member, splitting from the party in 1912 on tactical grounds. In 1913, the Florida Colored Baptist Convention carefully discussed socialism and offered its endorsement. A. Phillip Randolph and Chandler Owen founded the black socialist periodical *The Messenger.* As the black migration northward grew, so too grew the concern of many socialists for the black struggle.

The Communist Party of America would also count among its ranks major black and women leaders. It is claimed, for instance, that W.E.B. DuBois died a communist. The Communist Party developed an analysis of the black situation several generations ago called the "Black Belt" thesis. Similarly, the Communist Party drew to itself militant women leaders of the working class like Elizabeth Gurley Flynn, who led the Lawrence textile strike.

The great socialist hero of the era was undoubtedly Gene Debs. People thought of Abraham Lincoln when they saw this giant, gawky, Midwestern figure. A former locomotive fireman, Debs was to the fight against monopoly what Lincoln was to the fight against slavery. He always struck a populist note in his language, as in his saying, "When I rise it will be with the ranks and not from the ranks." Originally politically conservative—opposed to strikes, government ownership, and class conflict—Debs radically shifted under attack from the industrialists and their government power. Twice imprisoned, he eventually abandoned the Democratic Party, led major strikes, and in his bid for president proclaimed himself a socialist.

> The issue is socialism versus capitalism. I am for socialism because I am for humanity. We have been cursed with the reign of gold long enough. Money constitutes no proper basis of civilization. The time has come to regenerate society—we are on the eve of universal change.[42]

Out of the labor struggles—weakened by depressions, war, spies, agent provocateurs, armed force, and judicial undermining, as well as by racial, ethnic, and sexual divisions—the only major organization able to survive in strength was the AFL. Part of the price of its survival had been the official endorsement of capitalism. For the earlier 30 years of labor history, the two dominant organizations—the National Labor Union and the Knights of Labor—had demanded the replacement of the capitalist system by an economy owned and operated by the people. Perhaps understandably, the AFL did not.

The vision underlying much of AFL policy was charted by Samuel Gompers, who saw unions as partners with capital. The style came to be known as "business unionism" and was threatened with a tendency to protect the few workers at the expense of many, be they "unskilled," underemployed, or unemployed. As the narrow vision grew, the racial, ethnic, and sexual tensions within the American working class were further aggravated. The politics of Gompers linked him with the Progressive movement, which was adapting the American system to life under the big corporation, coupled with a strong neo-imperialist role in the world. This led to what William Appleman Williams has called a syndicalist structuring of American society, under the tripartite leadership of heads of unions, corporations, and government.[43] The theory was developed by Herbert Hoover, but implemented by Franklin Delano Roosevelt. Hoover's fear was that if the corporations alone had the power, there would be fascism; if labor alone had it, there would be socialism; and if government alone had it, there would be tyranny. While the theory is neat, the reality often became a pyramid where the corporations dominated and government served as its handmaid, while labor was at the bottom.

There was strong resistance from the IWW to the narrow course charted by Gompers. Mother Jones supported the IWW ("Wobblies") as did Thomas Haggerty, a Catholic priest who drafted the preamble to its founding document. The 1905 IWW call to its founding convention leveled a direct attack on the limitations of the craft-union tendencies:

> Universal economic evils afflicting the working class can be eradicated only by a universal working-class movement. Such a movement of the working class is impossible while separate craft and wage agreements are made favoring the employer against other crafts in the same industry, and while energies are wasted in fruitless jurisdictional struggles which serve only to further the personal aggrandizement of union officials.[44]

Primarily for the unskilled and unorganized, the IWW brought together migrant workers, outlawed members from other unions, lumberjacks, cowboys, and farm hands. Legendary figures rose up in the IWW—poets and singers like Joe Hill, the Swede later executed by the State of Utah; "Big" Bill Haywood, leader of the famous Cripple Creek strike; Elizabeth Gurley Flynn, the famous young woman organizer; and experienced labor leaders like Joseph Ettor and Arturo Giovannitti, also a poet. The IWW's most famous strike was against Lawrence Textiles in

1912, where 23,000 textile workers struck. Elizabeth Flynn quickly emerged as their leader. In the words of Mary Heaton Vorse,

> When Elizabeth spoke, the excitement of the strikers became a visible thing. She stood up there, young, with her Irish blue eyes, her face magnolia white, and her cloud of black hair, the very picture of a youthful revolutionary girl leader. . . . It was as though a spurt of flame had gone through the audience, something stirring and powerful, a feeling which has made the liberation of people possible.[45]

Many workers were jailed and beaten during the strike. Ettor and Giovannitti were arrested on a framed-up murder charge, and Elizabeth Gurley Flynn was imprisoned many years later, at 62 years of age, as a communist violating the Smith Act.

Because so much of the white labor militancy had been inspired by foreign-born workers, particularly Irish and Italian, labor struggles were branded un-American or the work of foreign agents. Such sentiments had operated strongly when 19 Irish miners were sentenced to death for their "conspiratorial" role in the Molly McGuires, an alleged inner circle of the Ancient Order of Hibernians. Similar sentiments arose in the famous case of Bartolomeo Vanzetti and Nicola Sacco, two immigrant radicals blamed for a payroll robbery. The case really had nothing to do with the alleged crime but was rather a political and ethnic trial. Judge Webster Thayer, who presided over the trial, remarked privately that it was necessary to protect the country from "reds" and referred to the defendants as "those anarchist bastards." Both Sacco and Vanzetti were sentenced to death and electrocuted in August 1927.

In the meantime the Progressive movement tried to steer the country away from socialist influences. "Ford, not Marx" became the rallying cry of increased production and worker speed-ups. Even Al Capone, foretelling subsequent collaboration between the US Central Intelligence Agency (CIA) and the multi-ethnic crime syndicates, warned that "we must keep the worker away from red literature and red ruses."[46] Despite Capone's "patriotic" admonitions, Italian communities on both sides of the Atlantic mourned quietly on the night of the Sacco and Vanzetti executions. Hours before dying, Sacco wrote a letter to his son Dante:

> So, Son, instead of crying be strong, so as to be able to comfort your mother, and when you want to distract your mother from the discouraging soulness, I will tell you what I used to do. Take her for a long walk in the quiet country, gathering wild flowers here and there, resting under the shade trees, between the harmony of the vivid stream and the gentle tranquility of mother-nature, and I am sure she will enjoy this very much as you surely would be happy for it. But remember always, Dante, in the play of happiness, don't use yourself only. . .help the weak ones that cry for help, help the persecuted and the victims because they are your better friends; they are the comrades that fight and fall as your father and Bartolomeo fought and fell. . . . for the conquest of the joy of freedom for all.[47]

The great movement to protect the nation from foreign influences was also the instrument of the agent of anti-black terror in the South, namely the KKK. Claiming itself 100% American, the Klan was against blacks, trade unions, communism, Roman Catholics, and Jews. How strange that a nation made up almost entirely of immigrant peoples should cast as its worst curse "foreign," while the truly native peoples (Indians) have been the object of genocide for several centuries. Even the women's suffrage movement, born in great sympathy for both abolitionism and socialism, found much of its middle-class sectors led into a political alliance against the foreign-born and against freed blacks.

But the Progressive era and business unionism hardly brought peace or prosperity. Testimony before the La Follette Committee showed that even as late as 1934, American industry was spending $80 million yearly to hire spies whose task was to break union power. General Motors alone spent over $400,000 for Pinkerton spies between January 1934 and July 1936. Similarly, American industry was spending hundreds of thousands of dollars each year for tear gas, automatic pistols, armored cars, fragmentation bombs, and submachine guns.

In response to renewed pressures, labor solidarity and militancy began to emerge again. The general strike in San Francisco in the summer of 1934 marked the fresh climate. Mike Quin, historian of the strike, records how the power of labor was apparent:

> Labor had withdrawn its hand. The workers had drained out of the shops and plants like life-blood, leaving only a silent framework embodying millions of dollars worth of invested capital. In the absence of labor, the giant machinery loomed as so much idle junk....[48]

In 1936 the CIO was born, the expression of the old fighting spirit. Growing out of critical forces within the AFL, it soon split the conservative leadership. For the first time in the century, it organized thousands of black workers on a basis of equality into the industrial unions. The potential power of white-black labor unity was quickly perceived, and CIO men and women were flogged, tarred and feathered, and even killed by the KKK for organizing in the South.

The success of John L. Lewis' CIO and its later direction by Philip Murray were due in part to the strong presence of Communist Party members within its ranks. Originally, Lewis and Murray did not examine party affiliation, only loyalty to the workers and to the CIO's principle, "Organize the Unorganized." While the communist presence was certain, voices like Cardinal Mundelein's of Chicago warned against using it as a pretext for injustice.

> Don't let others use communism as a cloak to cover corrupt practices when they cry out against communism, and they themselves practice social injustice; when they fight against a minimum wage and we find girls and women trying to live on ten and fifteen cents an hour.[49]

As a result of worker solidarity and resistance against "red-baiting," the CIO grew by 1945 to six million members.

When the "hot" World War II was over, the Cold War began, both against the Soviet Union and against leftist tendencies in the labor movement. C.E. Wilson of General Electric was at least frank in declaring that the Cold War had two targets, the American labor movement at home and the Soviet Union abroad. Under attack the CIO split into center and left camps. The communist-dominated unions were cast out by the center. While American communists seemed uncritical of totalitarian tendencies in the Russian system, the center wing lost its critical sense at home. Philip Murray wrote in 1948, "We have no classes in this country. . . . We are all workers here."[50] That was a reverse phrasing of "What's good for GM is good for the country."

Among the three main forces of America's working people—small farmers, the black freedom movement, and the predominately white unions—there were strong *religious* divisions.

A populist Protestantism continued to nourish the white rural and Midwestern section, growing out of the frontier churches which had sprung up relatively free of upper-class and clerical control. This Protestantism was very different from that of the urban, middle-class churches of the establishment.

The most noticed Protestant presence, however, came from the liberal leadership of the middle-class churches. The leadership of this sector later fell to Reinhold Niebuhr. As a young pastor in the midst of Detroit's industrialism, he had been drawn to socialist currents and even founded with others the recently revived journal *Radical Religion*. By 1940, however, Niebuhr had become disillusioned and abandoned the Socialist Party. He later became a religious chaplain to the liberal strategies of the Cold War era, strategies whose exploitative face would be clearly revealed in the 1960s and 1970s.

The earlier Social Gospel movement, on which Niebuhr drew in part, yet later reacted against, had nourished many separate ideological currents.[51] Some Social Gospel leaders, such as Washington Gladden, Shailer Matthews, and Raymond Robins, were apprehensive about socialism and class conflict. They stressed instead individual conversion and moral suasion. Others, such as Walter Rauschenbusch and Harry F. Ward, pressed toward a systemic critique of American capitalism and viewed more favorably socialist theories, although they kept their distance from socialist parties. A Christian turn toward class struggle and cooperation with socialist parties came in the figure of George Herron. Early on he supported the Socialist Labor Party and later worked with Eugene Debs' Social Democratic Party. He was instrumental in merging elements of both into the Socialist Party of America. Bob Craig remarks,

> Herron's entrance into the socialist movement marked a change in the subsequent course of Christian socialism in that most Christian

socialists were thereafter directly affiliated with socialist parties.[52]

Black Christianity followed the sufferings of the freed slaves through sharecropping and tenant-farming into living in the Northern ghettos. While closer to the white populist Protestanism than to the middle-class version, it was kept severely segregated from its white cousin and nurtured a strong prophetic and eschatological strain. Black Christianity would offer a prophetic challenge to all the American people. From that flower in turn would emerge the major critical strands of theology in the American theological tradition, namely, the various currents of Black Theology.

The vision of Black Christianity, although particularist in its roots and expression, remains perhaps one of the strongest sources for redemption of the American Dream. In that sense the vision of Black Theology is a universal vision. Its fresh construction of the American Dream perhaps reached its greatest flower, born of the thorns of suffering and on the eve of still deeper suffering, in the preaching of Martin Luther King, Jr. He, who had been to the mountain which overlooked America's cross, could still tell the nation's people of the dream's promise which lay ahead.

The dominant religion of the union movement was Catholicism. Still under the post-Reformation freeze, Catholic structures and ritual continued in the shape given them by the old European landed aristocracy. There was a populist element in Catholic pietism, but this came from an agrarian past and withered before long in the urban, industrial environment. Furthermore, the alien and hostile Protestant culture made the Catholic tradition only more rigid and defensive, as Protestantism was equated with those who controlled the society.

Because of its closeness to the labor movement, the Catholic church became organized labor's unofficial religious chaplain. At home with power, but nervous about class conflict, the Catholic influence reacted negatively to leftist strains in the movement and later became a major force in assisting the Cold War, both internally and externally. It was partly because of their usefulness in the Cold War struggle against socialist forces at home and abroad that Catholic leaders were taken into the confidence of the American upper classes. The Vatican-Washington connection, rather than threatening American power, proved very helpful in strengthening it. Catholic historian John Tracy Ellis quotes an anticlerical liberal historian:

> Separation between church and state is a basic tenet of liberation. But today Catholicism is possibly the greatest force checking the spread of communism in the Western World. . . . On the borders of the communist empire, what holds West Germans, Italians, and Filipinos against communism is not so much love for liberty and for democracy, or even independence, as the Catholic church. Necessity dictates cooperation between the American nation and the Catholic and other churches.[53]

Within American Catholicism, the Irish voices dominated, moving strongly into hierarchical authority and upward mobility. Non-Irish "white ethnic" Catholicism would in turn be kept in place by Irish American power brokers in church, labor, and the Democratic Party.

The dulling of the critical edge toward fundamental social change within Catholicism and the other churches coincided with the growth of the American middle class—a requirement of the expanding technical and professional base of American capitalism. This upward mobility was no miraculous characteristic of the American way of life. It was simply a function of the period of expanding capitalism at the zenith of American global power. (That day now seems over, but the story belongs more properly to our next section.)

The structural tragedy of these heroic struggles of America's working peoples was that they remained so separate. The rich ethnic and racial diversity, the broad geographic and economic expanses to be filled, the basic sexual division, the resistance to a critical examination of foreign policy, and the strong religious antagonisms all left the potential forces for justice in disarray. Many came together in temporary and fragile coalition during the New Deal, but the underlying social theory was weak and lent itself to frustration and co-optation and really required a world war to get the nation moving again. In turn the American Left, the only force capable of providing a theoretical framework for the integration of the multiple social struggles, proved incapable of creating a unified and broad political force. Eventually isolated, without the support of labor, of peoples of color, or of the women's movement, it became the victim of the McCarthy era and was briefly forgotten.

Without a coherent social theory and a firm practical alliance, the distinct social movements in America had faced their battles for the most part in isolation. Separate screws were turned upon white unions, the black freedom movement, small farmers, women, and the American Left. The four major issues of injustice in America—class oppression, racism, sexism, and imperialism—were not systemically linked in popular consciousness.

Throughout the period of expansion, each of these separate issues went through a qualitative shift. In the early years of expansion, blacks were still slaves and their struggle was one for freedom. After freedom had been gained, however, the struggle shifted to one of tenant farmers, sharecroppers, migrant workers, and (later) a Northern urban proletariat functioning as an industrial-reserve army, played off against white workers and doing the society's menial work. The white labor movement, whose original struggle had been simply to organize, now had to come to terms with the powerful organization it had created, the leaders of which would be tempted simply to join hands with other men of power in the society. While organization was still a major need (as many as 80% of American workers remaining unorganized), the power of the movement would have to struggle between conservative, liberal, and radical social visions. Working-class women, at first the prisoners of the home, were drawn into the factories, shops, and offices (and still burdened with household work), while middle- and upper-class women were molded into a combination of giant consumer and object of sexual consumption themselves. The images of Hollywood and Madison Avenue became the model for women across the world and at home. Middle- and upper-class women were supplied with beauty magazines and housekeeping magazines illustrating how they could shape themselves into this model, while lower-class women were given gossip and movie magazines so that they could vicariously enter that world. Finally, the imperialist outreach shifted from the overt conquest of land to neo-colonial economic penetration. The style had shifted from mercantilism to corporate and consumer capitalism.

It is perhaps understandable that these major social movements could not come together to create an interdependent consciousness with a systemic criticism. The nation was still very young, bringing in new people every year. Its internal structures were changing more rapidly than any social movement could follow. The transportation and communications links were weak across the broad continent. The American Left was rooted in European struggles and still searching for an adequate theory of racism and sexism, as well as having little creative appreciation of the power of culture and religious consciousness. In addition, American capitalism was still expanding and able to sustain major depressions without having its power undercut. This continuing expansion was able to cream off the top leadership of the major movements and accommodate them in the society. Looking back, therefore, it seems that despite the struggles and failures, the objective conditions for a broad, unified, and radical social movement in America were not yet present.

The closest thing to an overarching political force of America's laboring people was the Democratic Party. But while this party had its greatest strength in the multi-racial and multi-ethnic working class, it was really a cross-class party. Especially in its leadership, it welcomed the more progressive Northern capitalist forces and Southern reactionary elites. It also developed, during the later Cold War years, close ties to American militarism. In many ways, the foreign policies of American imperialism came out of bipartisan consensus.

Close ties grew up among sectors of Democratic leadership and between them and the AFL-CIO around the support of neo-imperialism. The Alliance for Progress in Latin America, for instance, has been interpreted by many secular and religious Latin critics as a neo-imperialist enterprise. They have charged that certain sectors of the AFL-CIO cooperated closely with the CIA and other members of the intelligence community to fight socialist currents in foreign labor movements. Where existing unions could not be controlled, parallel unions were formed. The strategy grew out of the designs of Jay Lovestone, for many years director of the AFL-CIO's International Department. (Lovestone had been, in the 1920s, General Secretary of the Communist Party USA but in reaction to Stalinism turned into a militant anti-communist.) It became most aggressive with the creation of the American Institute for Free Labor Development (AIFLD), founded in 1962 in the wake of the Cuban Revolution.[54] Though many members and staff of the AFL-CIO were hardly aware of it, their organization was being perceived by workers in other countries as an agent of US imperialism. Even the Catholic trade-union movement in Canada kept a hostile distance from its southern neighbor for those very reasons.

Several important social groups were kept fairly hidden toward the end of this period. The Native Americans who survived the genocidal attack were herded away to reservations or ignored in urban areas. The Latins who were living in quiet poverty functioned as super-exploited farmworkers, together with the black rural proletariat. The poor whites of Protestant subcultures, although the subject of literary attention earlier on, were simply forgotten, as in Appalachia, where the mines shut down. And finally, with the successful entry of some American Catholics into the circles of relative power and affluence, many did not notice that all did not enter; those of Southern and East European ancestry especially, but also many of Irish and German heritage, still lived in great economic insecurity and often poverty.

America came together in the Second World War—but prematurely, because the unity pushed aside all issues of exploitation. The single national purpose, together with the global power and more generalized prosperity it later brought, gave the nation a sense of eternal strength and stability. America had saved Europe from fascism, and many had given their lives heroically for that task. It then turned in the Marshall Plan to reconstruct Europe and aided Japan significantly. The Food for Peace Program was soon distributing American agricultural surpluses to the world's hungry. America became the symbol of freedom, prosperity, and generosity. It was on top of the world. The nation would coast on its postwar euphoria and expansion for nearly two decades, until in the 1960s great cracks appeared in the foundation—and in the 1970s, great questions.

To summarize the expansion period, we see a young nation exploding upon the world. Its economic growth from a small cluster of agricultural and trading colonies to the world's giant of productivity occurred in less than 200 years, most of it in less than 80 years. Peoples of every color, from every continent, flocked to its shores, both voluntarily and involuntarily. In turn, the young nation reached out to the world for raw materials and for markets. Its massive economic growth, however, was marked by great exploitation both of its own people and of other peoples of the world. Genocide against the native peoples, enslavement of Africans, and harsh exploitation of white laborers had been one side of expansion's brutality. Neo-imperialist control of foreign peoples and their territories, especially in Latin America and Asia, had been the other side. Yet accompanying expansion's exploitation at every turn was broad but uncoordinated resistance—in the Indian wars, in the black freedom movement, in the union battles, and in the women's movement. The United States grew simultaneously rich in exploitation and in popular struggle against that exploitation.

Yet, politically, the objective conditions for a fundamentally critical and unified movement of working-class peoples seem not to have been present. The racial, ethnic, sexual, functional, religious, and regional divisions of America's working class were still sharp. The nation remained yet an untamed giant, both in land mass and population. The cultural dream of upward mobility nurtured a psychology of escape. The political and economic institutions, structured around bargaining which accommodated reform across class lines, undercut working-class unity. All these factors, and probably countless others, created what must remain the central paradox for those who try to take Marx's thought seriously in the American context. The paradox is that the world's largest capitalist nation, continually immersed in brutal social struggles, contained a labor force which has not yet established a class orientation, neither in its way of thinking nor in its way of doing politics.

The structural direction set by the early colonial elite was successful, namely, the design of a formally democratic system of "checks and balances" against class threats, together with expansionist economic policies. So long as economic expansion continued (both territorial and technological), it acted as a safety valve to release threatening social pressures. In turn the political system could continue to accommodate or undercut social protest by selective bargaining across class lines and by manipulation of checks and balances, as well as by producing the goods for a large number of workers. The structural design would run into trouble only when the frontier vanished. That brings us to the third period of American history.

III. America's Maturity: Limits and Crises [1]

American capitalism has entered into a systemic crisis, pressing it to a new structural stage in its development. This stage, the guiding policies of which have yet to be worked out, has been described negatively as the end of the post-World War II era and positively as the Age of Interdependence. However one describes it, the stage stands in contrast to the prior history of American capitalism, because it marks the gradual contraction of the American empire. Further, because the defusing of class struggle within the society previously depended on continued external expansion, the new stage could shake the American social system to its foundations. With the escape valves of territorial frontiers and internal upward mobility gone, the social system will probably be forced to redesign its economic, political, and cultural institutions.

Such redesign could gravitate toward either of two alternatives. The first would salvage the power of the controlling classes by a more authoritarian and exploitative capitalism. This pole, in turn, could either build on the interdependence of a diffused international capitalism, or on the independence of the American system, or something in between. In any case, the system probably would be pushed to authoritarian and exploitative policies. The second alternative would be a socialist challenge to the new stage of capitalism. This alternative also contains distinct possibilities, corresponding to the wide variety of interpretations within the fertile but divided American Left.

The two alternatives [2]—a more authoritarian, more exploitative capitalism or a socialist challenge—would be contemporary expressions of the contending interpretations of democracy in the foundational period—property rights versus human rights. In the maturity of the American experience, as distinguished from its prior history of expansion, the conflict between these two interpretations presses to the nature of the social system itself.

A. Outer Limits: The Crisis of Foreign Policy

The post-World War II period saw the climax and triumph of the expansionary thrusts of the American empire. The dynamic which created this triumph, however, eventually destabilized the world capitalist system and the United States as well.[3]

In less than 200 years, what began as a small, isolated nation emerged as the economic, political, and cultural leader of world capitalism both in the industrialized First World and in the post-colonial Third World. Official foreign policy documents refer to this period as the era of United States predominance; Marxists refer to it as the era of United States hegemony. The content is the same.

The economic leadership of the United States was acknowledged in the monetary arrangements of the major capitalist nations at the Bretton Woods conference in 1944. In the era of predominance, American banking and external investment expanded dramatically. (Total US direct investment abroad reached more than $70 billion by 1970.)

Politically, the old French and British military networks were replaced by US-centered alliances such as the North Atlantic Treaty Organization (NATO), the Southeast Asia Treaty Organization (SEATO), and the Central Treaty Organization (CENTO), and the United States set up an international police force designed to maintain law and order (i.e., security for investments) throughout the capitalist world. American military policies sought to contain and harass world socialism (the Cold War). In the diplomatic arena, the United States was able to dominate the United Nations (unless the Soviets used their veto in the Security Council).

Culturally, through the explosion of transportation and communications networks, many American values and ways of life—particularly the dress and music of middle-class youth—were carried to most of the world. American informality and problem-solving pragmatism made strong impacts in all sectors. American religious missionary efforts in the Third World also gained strength in this climate.

The destabilization precipitated by the postwar expansion expresses itself in *three structural threats* to American capitalism—one from the major industrial powers of world capitalism (Western Europe and Japan), one from the developing Third World, and one from the socialist world. In every case these threats are economic, political (including military), and cultural.

1. The First World: Industrial Capitalisms in Renewed Competition

The industrial capacity of Western Europe and Japan had been devastated by World War II, while US production was strengthened by the war effort. As a defense against the Soviets, however, the United States was required to rebuild both the Western European and Japanese economies, which it did with great capital outlays through programs such as the Marshall Plan. Had it failed to do that, the socialist movement within Europe and Asia would probably have made major gains. (In postwar Europe, for instance, the communist parties were very strong because of their resistance to fascism.) The rebuilding of the Western European and Japanese economies created strategic buffers against the Soviet Union and China, but these buffers eventually became economically competitive with the United States itself. This competition was even further complicated by the fact that many times it was American capitalist investments in Europe and Japan (especially in automobiles and electronics) which were competing with American-based industry and costing American workers their jobs. In addition to direct financial subsidies such as the Marshall Plan, the United States also bore much of the defense costs of its European and Japanese allies, enabling them to devote their energies to non-military production, while the United States labored under the costs of a global military empire. Further, the United States even underwrote the colonial wars of France and Portugal and directly took over the former in Indochina (Vietnam).

The threat from the First World eventually led to the breakdown of the international monetary system established at Bretton Woods in 1944. With the revival of international capitalism, an overvalued dollar made US-produced goods less competitive. Further, the deficit financing of the US war in Southeast Asia aggravated international inflation and weakened the dollar. Domestically, the United States experienced chronic deficit balance of payments; internationally, other nations resisted the American attempt to export inflation. This led to two devaluations of the dollar and finally to the elimination of the dollar as the standard world currency in the new monetary agreements reached in Jamaica in January 1976. In the new situation, the United States has corrected its deficit balance of payments and remains the strongest economy in the world, but its world economic power has been reduced.

Further, United States capitalism is caught in the split between requirements of its expansion into European and Japanese industry and its domestic self-interest. On the one hand, the foreign investments seem important for profit returns, because labor is cheaper outside the United States; on the other hand, if investments in foreign industry undercut the United States, there is a crisis at home.

The empire is also being weakened politically in the First World. Out of the severe economic recession of the 1970s, political instability grows in Europe. Western European communist parties are again aiming for power in one way or other, something which has not been a real possibility since the end of World War II. Further, the parties of Italy, Spain, France, and perhaps even Portugal, are beginning to set out on autonomous paths despite considerable tensions with Moscow. Some speak of the possibility of a "third socialist bloc" of Western Europe, subservient neither to Russia nor to China, but perhaps drawing Eastern Europe away from Russia and into a broad European alliance. Finally, they are attempting to integrate their socialist vision with the contributions of Western democratic ideals. This is leading to left/center coalitions between communists and socialists, in contrast to the center/right coalitions which dominated the postwar politics of Western Europe. Recently the Italian Communist Party moved to within a few points of the percentage held by the Christian Democratic Party (which has governed Italy through the postwar period), and in recent regional elections in Italy some 90% of all young people voted for the CPI. François Mitterand, the French socialist leader, speaks of these new movements as the emergence of a distinctly "Latin Socialism." All these events, of course, threaten to weaken the most important military alliance of the American empire, namely, NATO.

In Japan, too, the situation is not stable. Japan, like the United States, is seeking a triangular relationship with the USSR and China. Japan also faces considerable internal threat from a growing socialist movement. The Japanese Communist Party, long before those in Western Europe, defined itself as independent of Moscow and Peking and set out to integrate its socialist vision with Western notions of democracy. Again, in the post-Vietnam period, the United States finds itself searching for a new Asian policy.

Culturally, the leadership of the United States has also been weakened in the First World. Often there is deep prejudice against America and its policies, and this not only from the Left but from broad sectors of the populace. While being an American in the postwar period meant one was tantamount to being a hero, now many Americans find themselves, rightly or wrongly, apologizing for their nationality or defending it from hostile attack.

Hence, the American empire, in the very triumph of its First World predominance (or hegemony), laid the seeds for its weakening. The military buffers it created to defend its economic and strategic interests have become dangerous economic competitors and shaky strategic allies. Beneath all this, American capitalism, which created the empire, has become transnational in character and often operates in blatant opposition to the economic self-interest of the people of the United States. Finally, the United States finds itself suspected, resented, and even ridiculed among those who formerly were its closest friends.

2. The Third World: Multinational Corporations and a North/South Confrontation

The Third World includes the developing nations of Asia, Africa, and Latin America. Its role has always been central in the development of the American empire. The first capital accumulation of America was founded on the human plunder of Africa for slaves during early mercantile capitalism. Special claim was laid to Latin America by the Monroe Doctrine and subsequent imperialist interpretations of it. And finally, outreach to Asia was the logical development of westward expansion on the North American continent. In the present structural stage, the Third World offers the greatest financial opportunities for transnational capitalism but at the same time precipitates the greatest destabilization of the world system.

To understand why this is so, it is necessary to examine the new structural model evolving in the relation between the First World and the Third World. Marxists have interpreted the First World/Third World relationship as one of imperialism, from the earliest colonizations by Western Europe to the neo-colonial (primarily economic, and not overtly political) structures of the post-World War II era. The relation between the two worlds is spoken of as the relationship between the center and periphery of a single international economic system.

In the classic imperialist model, the periphery provided cheap raw materials and lucrative markets for finished products, while the center of the system provided the industrial base for the production of finished products, as well as its own internal markets. The cheap raw materials and lucrative markets were seen as providing financial subsidies to the system's center, part of which underwrote a higher standard of living for large sectors in the nations of the center, and part of which provided the surplus capital for further expansion of the system, both internally and externally.

In the present situation, however, many Marxist analysts see a dramatic shift in the center/periphery relationship. In the new model, both the center and the periphery are undergoing fundamental changes internally and in relation to each other. The central actor in this shift is the transnational corporation.[4]

Much of the classical production apparatus of Western Europe, Japan, and North America has begun to shift to a Third World base. This began gradually in the early postwar era in the form of "import substitution." This meant that the transnationals began to produce, within Third World nations, products for domestic consumption which these nations had formerly imported from the First World. Much of the production, however, was not domestically owned by a national capitalist class, although they were a factor, but by transnational capital from Western Europe, North America, or Japan. Frequently, First World "development programs" or foreign aid subsidized this penetration of Third World economies.

The import-substitution phase was not seen as a threat by American labor, because it meant primarily developing new markets rather than stealing old ones. Thus, as mentioned before, the AFL-CIO cooperated with the US Agency for International Development (USAID) and the American-based businesses active in Latin America through the AIFLD, with close ties to Christian Democratic parties in Latin America. The goal of the program was to foster solidarity between US and Latin American workers in a single anti-communist labor movement. The program backfired, however, but more for political than economic reasons. As political polarizations heightened in Latin America, AIFLD found itself in deep conflict with the strong leftist forces in Latin American unions. (Lately AIFLD has been accused of being deeply penetrated by the CIA and of active involvement, even to the point of providing leadership, in several rightist coups throughout Latin America.[5] As a result, there is widespread suspicion of ties between the AFL-CIO and the CIA throughout Latin America. Rather than encouraging worker solidarity, the AIFLD program may have further isolated American labor. But the issues remained political, not economic. Only in the next stage of development of transnational capitalism would economic issues become crucial.)

Quickly the transnational corporations moved from the simple import-substitution phase to what some call the "export platform" phase. This means that the transnationals were not simply producing in the Third World for internal markets but that they were using Third World countries as productive bases for export back to the First World. Thus, American capital not only invested in Japanese and German auto production, in competition with its own US production facilities; it also moved production to the Third World. This trend can be documented especially in the textiles and electronics sectors. Organized labor refers to this phenomenon as the "international runaway shop." While there are many factors involved in the shift, one of the strongest seems to be the search for cheap labor. Ironically, not only were the transnationals (about 75% of which are American-based) abandoning their national base and exporting American jobs in the process but they were also being richly subsidized by the American taxpayer. Recent studies have pointed both to the domestic job loss and to the tax incentives offered to corporations which go abroad.[6] This phenomenon of international runaway shops, or the transnational corporation, is making foreign-policy questions the most important ones for the American labor movement. Different from the American labor stake in the foreign policy of the Cold War period, which was political, the stake now becomes economic.*

The effect of the new structural situation deeply destabilizes the system both in its center and in its periphery.

At the center, the First World workers feel a triple pressure. First, they lose jobs from the export of production to areas of cheaper labor. Second, they find that retraining and adjustment assistance are meaningless, for there are too few new jobs—a situation resulting from the fact that the system's center begins to abandon classical industries

---

*In another sense, the stake of the US labor movement in the foreign policy of the Cold War was also economic. World War II and the military-oriented postwar economy provided many defense jobs, especially for skilled workers who were unionized.

and concentrate instead on the highly capital-intensive frontier or complex technology, which the periphery simply cannot handle. (Much of this frontier and complex technology is military-related, so that the military sector grows as a key factor in American production, perpetuating the war orientation of the economy. Even this status is undermined, however, by the export of vital technologies to the Soviet Union, which may bolster political "détente" but in fact undermines the uniqueness of American technology.) The stress on capital-intensive technology begins to invade all sectors of American production as an effort to cut production costs. This phenomenon covers a wide range of jobs—from agriculture, where production is increasing but the numbers of employees and small farmers is decreasing under the growth of agribusiness, to newspaper production (as is evidenced in the pressmen's strike at *The Washington Post*). Third, with what jobs remain, there are strong pressures to "cut production costs" (i.e., reduce workers' share) in order to make American labor more competitive in the international market. Ironically, countries controlled by rightist governments, such as South Korea and Brazil, which were created partially out of the political purposes of the old Cold War, are becoming havens for the runaway shops which now cost American workers their jobs.

The new structural situation also destabilizes the periphery of the system. The penetration of transnational capital follows a development model which gives priority to profit maximization within an international system. This process of "rationalization" manipulates all the parts around the profit motive and never deals with national economies in a holistic way. As a result, several disruptive processes are unleashed.

The model concentrates in the Third World on urban industrial development which depresses agriculture and generates massive peasant migrations to the urban centers. In this sense, the urban/rural relation is a microcosm of the center/periphery relation in the classical model of imperialism. Because industrial development in the urban center is also capital-intensive, there are few jobs for the displaced peasants. This creates a giant population of urban marginals, slum dwellers, or *lumpenproletariat*, whatever one wishes to call them. Increasingly, the urban centers of the capitalist world are becoming centers of poverty and misery rather than centers of promise.

Within the rural sector of the Third World, the disruption attracts either transnational capital or large national capital to agribusiness styles of production. Because internal markets are usually weak due to poverty (great internal *need* not being reflected in market demand because of income scarcity), agribusiness in the Third World often orients itself to producing cash crops for export rather than growing food for domestic consumption. This orientation is, in the view of some, one of the central factors in the current world food crisis, wherein as many as 500 million persons suffer from severe malnutrition or starvation.[7] Thus, for example, while famine ravaged the Sahel recently, transnational agribusiness corporations were working some of the Sahel's most fertile lands to produce large cotton crops for export. This scene is a 20th-century repetition of the market-induced Irish famines of the 19th century.

In addition, the penetration of foreign capital brings with it Western lifestyles which stress conspicuous consumption in an environment of conspicuous misery. This creates deep alienation between masses and elites within many Third World nations, similar to the alienation generated within the First World between big business and ordinary people. The establishment media portrays the structural conflict between the Third World and America as *national* conflicts, but in many ways the elites from both sides/"worlds" are better integrated with each other than they are with the ordinary people of their own societies/worlds. The fight is not really between the ordinary people of both sides—for neither side will probably receive much from the battle—but among the elites to see who will get how much of the pie of privilege. Such destabilization in the system's periphery causes great political unrest, particularly when it brings with it the promise, but not the performance, of social improvement.

This progression has been dramatically illustrated in Latin America. There the penetration of transnational capital aroused great hope within the national middle classes that their nations were on the way to development. The penetration and expectations were stepped up strongly during the Kennedy years when, following the Cuban Revolution, it seemed possible to beat communism in Latin America by wiping out poverty, a concept which led to the formation of the Alliance for Progress. The Alliance, however, like its American domestic counterpart, the War Against Poverty, was never able to keep its promises. As a result, the system had to turn to tactics of repression to constrain social dissent. This signaled the breakdown of the positive face of the Cold War; in its place the negative face emerged. As it had in many other areas of the world, US foreign policy supported and virtually created right-wing dictatorships in order to guarantee stability for investments. While Cold War rhetoric in defense of democracy and freedom is still heard, it is increasingly hard to believe. The US government has become a staunch backer of repressive and exploitative governments throughout the Third World; in Latin America, it has been linked with rightist coups in Guatemala, British Guyana, the Dominican Republic, Brazil, Bolivia, Uruguay, and finally Chile.[8] The same phenomenon can be seen in the close relationships between the US government and the governments of South Africa and Iran, to mention only a few. In the Mediterranean world, fascist Greece and Spain were other right-wing friends of the Cold War campaign.

Again, the creation of authoritarian and exploitative Third World governments granted stability to capitalist development but also destabilized the political relation between the center and periphery. Together with socialist-oriented nations of the Third World, these new leaders have gathered into a global coalition to challenge First World hegemony over the international economic system. This movement has taken shape in the "Group of 77" (actually more than 100 nations) within the United Nations and is backed up by the economic clout of Third World cartels such as the Organization of Petroleum Exporting Countries (OPEC). Most recently, this coalition has challenged the old international economic order designed by the dominant Western capitalist nations out of World War II and has called for a "New International Economic Order."[9] This call has led to "producer-consumer dialogues" between the First World and the Third World and to the creation of new international monetary agreements no longer based on the US dollar.

The new spirit among the Third World nations has brought greater cultural unity to the peoples of color of the world, who make up the majority of its population. The spirit is also marked by a new nationalism which, while open to Western contributions, stresses autonomous cultural roots. How well these visions will stand up under capitalist development, however, remains an open question. National bourgeoisies have been very skilled at mustering nationalist and militant rhetoric to gain leverage for their narrow social classes in the international system, often to the detriment of their own populations. Furthermore, even though there is strong cultural unity within the Third World, and at least temporary political unity, there are also severe strains among the groups behind the New International Economic Order.

These strains, which the US government has tried unsuccessfully to exploit, are of two kinds.

First, there is the strain between the rich and poor nations within the coalition. The more affluent nations have won their wealth either from cartelization of their strategic resources (like oil) or from making somewhat skilled and controlled labor forces available at a low price to transnational capital (Taiwan or South Korea). The poorer nations, which lack both prized resources and ready labor pools, have been severely hurt by the current international inflation—flowing, it seems, from the Vietnam war and from giant increases in commodity prices both from the Third World and the First World. The US government has tried to exploit this division by threatening what some have called a "new" Cold War.[10]

In contrast to the "old" Cold War, a conflict which rotated on an East/West axis around political issues, this "new" one would swing on a North/South axis, on economic issues. In the old Cold War, it was communism versus capitalism; in the new Cold War, it would be food versus oil (and other strategic commodities). In the old Cold War, the threat was nuclear holocaust; in the new Cold War, it would be the holocaust of starvation for the world's poor. Many people believe that the US government, by using the food "weapon," can break the poorer nations (now sometimes called the "Fourth World") away from the rest of the Third World and thus destroy the coalition.

So far, this tactic has not been successful, because the Fourth World seems to perceive the rich First World as more dangerous to it than the rich Third World. (This Third World/Fourth World solidarity has been spoken of as the "trade-union model," the parameters of which dictate that some are willing to undergo great sacrifice in order to hold out for a fair deal in the future.) Further, the promise of American aid is viewed skeptically, because it is understood that the United States is now dependent on lucrative food sales to more affluent nations (such as the Soviet Union) in order to offset the deficit balance of payments, while what food *is* available for aid has been directed to some of the rich nations of the Third World for political rather than humanitarian uses (e.g., to Egypt vis-a-vis its position in the volatile Middle East). In addition, while the United States grants a fraction of 1% of its GNP to foreign aid (and even that seems to be shrinking), with complicated strings attached, several Arab nations have been granting about 8% of their GNP and may be increasing that. Clearly, much Arab aid has so far gone to other Arab or Muslim nations, and certainly there are strings attached (like denunciation of Zionism as a form of racism), but realistically the poor nations perceive with more hope opportunities for aid from the Arabs than from the West.

What probably really weakens the hand of the United States in its attempt to split the Fourth World from the Third World is its strategy in response to the second strain in the coalition, namely, the tension between "moderates" (e.g., Iran) and "radicals" (e.g., Algeria). The moderates in the coalition are apparently seeking entry into the club of rich Western nations rather than really challenging the West in fundamental fashion. The radicals, however, are seeking what might be called a world planning system, semi-socialist in nature, for the whole community. Naturally, the US government has sought to appease the moderates while isolating the radicals. The radicals' perspective, however, seems more beneficial to the Fourth World. Thus, in response to the first strain (rich/poor) in the coalition, the United States is trying to play the poor off against the rich; in response to the second strain (moderate/radical), it finds itself playing the rich off against the poor. If both strategies were equally weighted, they would simply neutralize each other, but the US position seems to be to play the poor off against the rich in public rhetoric, while conceding to the rich against the poor in real negotiations.

The question of how much the United States should accommodate itself in this second strategy is a source of great controversy among American elites. Responding to the question are basically two schools of thought, which are overlapping, namely, a confrontationist school and an accommodationist school. The controversy between the two accounts in part for vacillation within US policy. The confrontationist school, perhaps typified by the former US ambassador to the United Nations, Daniel Patrick Moynihan, has stressed a hard line, with US food as the weapon. The accommodationist school, perhaps typified by Ford's Under Secretary of State for Economic Affairs, Charles W. Robinson, has stressed a soft line of dialogue, some concessions, and aid for the Fourth World. The difference between the two schools is grounded in their different appraisals of America's role in transnational capitalism. The confrontationist school seems to stress the independent aspects of American capitalism, while the accommodationist school seems to stress the interdependent aspects.

While the confrontationist school may appear more "American" and "patriotic" than the accommodationist school, it seems that neither position will serve well the economic needs of the American people. In terms of domestic social policy, both would probably be obliged structurally to turn to a more authoritarian and exploitative capitalism at home, in order to keep the domestic subsystem buoyant and flexible within the international system. Indeed, many confrontationists, while clamoring for democracy abroad, are stressing the limits of democracy at home. They often appeal to the Federalist tradition of Alexander Hamilton against Jeffersonian populism. Despite the rhetoric, they would seem to defend the freedom of property against the freedom of people.

3. The Second World: End of the Cold War

In light of the fact that many social elites within the United States are stirring up a new wave of anti-communism at home while expanding diplomatic and economic exchange with communist nations, it is important to ask, What is the role of the communist nations in the present crisis?

The first fact, with respect to the communist nations, is that American foreign policy has dramatically shifted its relationship to them. Détente with the Soviet Union and President Richard M. Nixon's visit to China are the two most powerful expressions of this fact. However, the question arises, Why the dramatic change after the confrontationist mentality of two and a half decades of the Cold War? The official answer is the desire to reduce world tensions and to avoid nuclear holocaust. Undoubtedly such desires are an important element, but it seems that there are other factors operating, too. Among them are, first, the failure of the Cold War containment policies and, second, the competitive struggle for profit under transnational capitalism.

First, the Cold War strategies were unable to contain the spread of communism in the world.[11] The containment policies themselves portended the end of the expansionary period of the American empire, which then shifted its policies from the positive expansion of its own influence to the negative containment of a power it could not displace. In that sense, the American empire met its outer limit in the Soviet Union.

The containment policies of the Cold War received rather broad popular support at home for many reasons. One was that the Soviet Union had already entered its Stalinist phase, and many who had been enthusiastic about early accomplishments of the Russian Revolution became apprehensive about the concentration of power in the state and its party leadership. Second, many in the American working class, particularly its industrial sectors, had roots in Eastern Europe.

Eastern Europe has traditionally been a ground of struggle between the imperialist desires of East and West, reflected religiously by the triangle of religious power which surrounds it—namely, Rome, Constantinople, and Moscow, the three great patriarchies of Christianity. Within that triangle, the region is riddled with political and religious tensions. Within that triangle, too, Eastern European socialism came to power out of the struggle against German imperialism and in a strategic alliance with Russian might. Naturally, in the rigid confrontation of the Cold War, military alliance with Russian power meant Russian domination of Eastern European political life.

On the other side of the iron curtain a similar political domination took place in more subtle form, without the overt political repression of dissidents (although one could point to covert, especially economic, repression). Thus, in postwar Italy, although the Italian communists were very close to gaining control of Italian political life (by democratic means), a massive campaign was waged by those who held social power (including the religious sector) to place the Christian Democratic Party (CDP) in command. By massive financial aid and propaganda campaigns (secular and religious), supported by the intelligence forces of the United States, the Italian CDP was able to gain control. Until fairly recently, although a minority government, they have continued in power with relative security.

In the popular US consciousness, an overriding issue which led to the creation of the iron curtain was religious freedom. The development of just such a consciousness was in fact crucial for the strategically important Catholic support of the Cold War, both on the part of the Vatican and on the part of Slavic and Hungarian American Catholics in the industrial working class, as well as with the Irish American hierarchy. Christian leftists reviewing the Cold War heritage would be foolish to view the religious question in a reductionist manner, because there was a serious threat to religious freedom from the Left.

Catholics in the United States and Eastern Europe supported the church against socialism partly because their peasant roots were still strong and, consequently, their alienation from traditional Catholicism (which characterizes those who have lived several generations under industrial life) had not yet developed. Similarly, in the pre-Vatican II era, the feudal consciousness of Catholic leadership was still dominant. In the feudal consciousness, which is relatively static, religion as a source of consolation and even festive escape plays a central role (hence, the jarring contrast between the "fiesta" spirit and the stress on the realistic suffering of the Crucifixion in traditional Catholicism). The possibility of a structural alternative was not a factor in the religious imagination of traditional Catholicism, simply because it was not part of feudal social imagination.

In addition, under feudal patterns the Catholic church was able to link in symbiotic unity the religious imagination of the poor peasantry with that of the landed aristocracy. This link allied the church with the political strategies of the artistocracy, but it also functioned in service of the peasantry. Furthermore, in regions where heightened nationalism became an important defense against the territorial ambitions of neighboring powers (sectors of Eastern Europe against Moscow, or Ireland against England), religion served as a source of national unity, between elite and mass, against the threatening powers. These factors must be taken into account in explaining why the Catholic church, embracing industrial workers in the United States as well as poor peasants in Eastern Europe, became so hostile to socialist currents in the Cold War era.

Religious support for the Cold War mentality has recently been weakened also for many reasons. First, the reforms of Vatican II, which had been gestating through this century, ended the domination of feudal consciousness over Catholic life and pitched into contention the distinct streams of religious imagination emanating from the urban middle classes, the urban working classes, and the anti-colonial consciousness of the Third World. As a result, the Catholic institution is caught in an unstable transition which—so far at least—gives it little real political leverage in any direction. Second, we now have a second and third generation of white ethnic Catholics whose mindset has been shaped by industrial life and whose religious imagination no longer corresponds to the feudal consciousness. Third, with the Vatican's diplomatic opening to the East, a new strategy of religious resistance seems to be emerging within Eastern Europe—one that does not ground its precepts of religious freedom in the rejection of socialism but which turns to the socialist experience itself for resources which are helpful to formulating a defense of religious rights. Thus, for example, in Lithuania, where many youth (who did not grow up under church guidance) turned to the church from within the socialist experience, the Catholic political strategy invokes in its defense the Russian Constitution and the writings of Lenin.[12]

The main reason for the abandonment of the Cold War policies, however, was not immediately the shift in religious imagination but the clear failure to contain the communist movement, plus the tactical opportunities opened by the breakup of the communist monolith.

Simple statistics show how unsuccessful was the containment policy. Whereas at the end of World War II only 7% of the world's population and 18% of its land mass were under communist governments, by 1975 some 35% of the world's population and more than 25% of its land mass had communist governments.[13] In the history of this spread, the earliest shock was the victory of the Chinese Revolution. Containment in Korea occurred only at the price of partition of the nation. A later shock came with the Cuban Revolution's leftist turn and the creation of a communist nation only miles off the shores of Miami. Finally, the American defeat in Southeast Asia brought the period to a close.

But the major Western adversary in the Cold War not only failed to contain communism; it also failed to preserve democracy within the "liberal" world with which it was supposedly allied. The United States quickly yielded its commitment to democracy for strategic needs (e.g., in Greece, Spain, and Portugal). Later, it became willing to yield political democracy for economic needs, even when there was little at stake strategically. Thus, the Cold War in Latin America eventually led to a continent blanketed with repressive military dictatorships, the very antithesis of democracy, whose rise to power depended on US backing. So the Cold War led not to democracy but to dictatorship across the world. This pattern suggests what Marxists have claimed all along, that the fundamental US purpose was the defense not of political freedom but of the economic needs of the business elites of the American empire.

The breakup of the communist monolith made possible an alternative—but still profitable—strategy for transnational capitalism. With the emergence of independent communist movements, beginning with Tito's Yugoslavia and proliferating globally after the Sino-Soviet split, the United States and other capitalist powers were able to maneuver between communist nations. This maneuverability proved important in two ways. First, multinational corporations found Eastern Europe very attractive because of the cheap and stable labor markets provided there. Because productivity was not undercut by frequent strikes (partly because of party control of the labor movement) and because the standard of living was lower than in the West, labor costs were cheaper. Also, the strong communist governments provided the same social stability that transnational capital had enjoyed under rightist dictatorships which repressed the trade-union movement and forbade strikes.

The accommodation thus made appeared, of course, a great betrayal to those sectors of the American labor movement which were so supportive of the Cold War strategies. It was difficult enough to see American capital ally itself in the Third World with right-wing elites who then suppressed the free trade-union movement and drained off American jobs by the promise of cheap and "disciplined" labor pools. But it was outrageous to see American capital then turn to communist nations for the same reasons! In addition, it appeared still more outrageous to them to see American capitalists, trying to offset the deficit balance of payments created by the export of jobs in the first place, then begin to undercut even further the security of American working people by exporting food and technology to the Soviet Union.

The reflex reaction of the Cold War labor consciousness is, of course, to defend American jobs. But while certainly it can be agreed that a comprehensive strategy to defend American workers must be the foundation of any new vision for the American people, it is questionable that past policies can supply guidance in the new structural period.

Within the United Nations, both the Third World and the Second World (the communist powers) have joined in an anti-imperialist coalition directed chiefly against the United States. The coalition crosses ideological lines and serves different purposes for capitalist and socialist nations. The capitalist nations within the Third World (called "moderates") are simply seeking a bigger piece of the international capitalist system for themselves. The communist nations, although interested in trade advantages with the West, are also seeking to undermine the economic, military, and political hegemony of the United States. This coalition has coalesced in opposition to the economic and political predominance of the United States.

Thus we can see the crisis of contemporary American foreign policy embodied in assaults from three fronts—from the system's traditional allies, namely, the other major capitalist powers in the First World; from the system's former periphery in the Third World; and from the system's former enemy, the communist powers in the Second World. Ironically, this third threat—from the communist nations—comes not in political form, but in economic form.

But the central agent of disruption in all three cases is the multinational corporation or, from a more systemic view, the *maturing of transnational capitalism.*

While the coalition is directed against the rest of the First World also—Western Europe and Japan—they have not formed a solid bloc with the United States, partly because they are more dependent on natural resources and energy supplies from the Third World, but also because they, too, are structurally in competition with the United States. There have been some efforts to form a united bloc of the First World; for example, Kissinger unsuccessfully tried to muster consumer solidarity against OPEC, and leading transnational capitalists (at the instigation of David Rockefeller) formed the Trilateral Commission, linking elites and policy advisers from Japan, Western Europe, and the United States. The efforts of Western elites to preserve a measure of Western power in the face of international restructuring will, however, probably prove prejudicial to the First World working classes and even to the middle classes.

The result of this disruption can only be the gradual weakening of Western power in general and of the American empire in particular.

While the United States remains the world's strongest economy, it is now only one strong economy among others—a position that is a long way from its having been the hegemonic leader of the world capitalist system, as it was in the post-World War II era. Thus we come to an entirely new period in American foreign policy, one in which we witness the empire's decline, rather than its expansion.

An interesting cultural effect of the shrinking of Western power is a "relativizing" of Western religion in the global community. Christianity little by little ceases to reflect—at least in the cultural sphere—the arrogance of the West; for the first time in the post-colonial era, it is perhaps beginning to listen to the message of non-Christian traditions, including the secular religion of Marxism—especially from the peoples of Asia, Africa, and even the native peoples of the Americas.

B. Inner Limits: The Crisis of Domestic Policy

The structural crisis of American capitalism within the international system dramatically affects life at home. The domestic system is caught in two fundamental contradictions, which are related and mutually aggravating. The first contradiction is between the desire to maintain the empire and the incredible costs of doing so (the general crisis of imperialism). The second contradiction is between the promises of the domestic social system to its people and the structural inability to meet those promises (the social struggle within the system's center).

In past periods of American history, the expansion of the American empire had relieved the pressure on the internal contradictions of the domestic capitalist system; thus, an imperialist foreign policy became a foundation for liberal social policies at home. Now, however, the decline of the American empire pulls the rug out from under domestic liberalism. As a result the nation faces a crisis not only in foreign policy but in domestic policy as well. Further, *foreign policy now aggravates domestic social tensions.* Let us examine some aspects of this aggravation in the structural life—economic, political, and cultural—of contemporary American society.

1. Economic Life: End of the New Deal [14]

The first signal of crisis came in the early 1970s with a deficit balance of payment totaling over $10 billion for 1971 and 1972. There were many reasons for this deficit balance in the 1970s, but all were functions of foreign policy. First, jobs were being massively exported by international runaway shops, causing in turn a greater dependence on imports. Second, the growing cost of American military power—dramatically aggravated by the arms race, by the war in Vietnam,[15] and by inflation—was a severe capital drain. And third, the devaluation of the dollar, while making US goods more competitive abroad, raised the costs of maintaining a large standing army abroad, as well as the costs of foreign imports. More recently, and best known in the popular mind, the OPEC cartel used its clout to gain much higher prices for oil.

The higher oil costs were possible partly because the interests of major oil companies were linked to the world economic system as well as the US interests but also because, following the US defeat in Vietnam, political and economic offensives against American power became possible. And, of course, the United States was peculiarly vulnerable to oil power because its whole economy was structured around automobile production.

While the rising oil prices seemed outrageous, OPEC was only following a pattern taught it by US business, whose commodity prices in the international market skyrocketed well in advance of the oil prices. This was especially true of American food. (This nation controls more than half of the world's wheat trade, proportionately more than any Arab nation controls of oil. US food prices rose dramatically in the face of world hunger.)

Several policies seem to be emerging as a response to the serious deficit balance of payment. The first has been manipulation of the current recession, the deepest since the Great Depression of the 1930s. By allowing high rates of unemployment, by not controlling prices, and by restricting credit through a tight money policy, the federal government was able to decrease domestic consumption, thus decreasing US dependence on foreign imports. Partly for that reason, the United States was able to show an $11 billion trade surplus in 1975; but, as some economists have remarked, the trade surplus looked so good largely because the economy looked so bad.

There are, however, other long-range policies (aiming beyond the recession) which are being initiated in an attempt to give the US economy balance and flexibility in the international system. These include the shifting of production toward the export of food, arms, and advanced technology. Thus, US arms sales abroad, for the fiscal year ending in June 1975, totaled $12 billion, while foreign food sales (accounting for 20% of all US exports) totalled about $22 billion. Also moves are being initiated to have domestic coal and perhaps nuclear power replace foreign oil as the major US energy resources. In addition, there are attempts to cut troop strength abroad and to replace it with tactical nuclear weapons. All these maneuvers may relieve the trade imbalance, but they aggravate the world and domestic situation still further.

Food sales are turning into a "weapon" that the United States threatens to use as blackmail against those nations which do not agree with its positions. One spokesperson recently alluded to a "zap list" being developed for US foreign-policy purposes. The zap list, however, will not include those powerful nations which strategically cannot be offended (e.g., Egypt) even if they refuse to accept US domination. So it becomes a "bully's list" against little, poor nations. The knowledge that such ideas are even contemplated heightens the already strong anti-American feeling in the world and further isolates the US from the world community.

Arms sales, of course, are particularly disruptive in an already tense world. But the US is not alone in its trafficking in this area; both the European community and the Soviet Union are also major arms dealers.

The possible shift to coal as a major energy source, while not unreasonable in the abstract, will apparently show little concern for human or ecological rights. The strip-mining of coal, both in Appalachia and in the West, is threatening to the human settlements which stand in their way. In the West, it is a direct attack on the lands of the American Indians, already pushed to the furthest margins of this society. In Appalachia, the stripped land will frequently not be able to be reclaimed or will be poorly reclaimed, perhaps threatening the creation of a desert in the eastern United States. Further, in mining operations, the drive for profit will apparently erode both worker-safety practices and ecological restrictions in all of industrial life. This is because a redesigned national system which formerly gained much of its profits from the structures of imperialism (trade, as well as the artificial power of the dollar) will have to turn more of its exploitative face inwards—against its own people. This turn is not the arbitrary choice of more malicious elites but the structural imperative of the new situation.

This turn of exploitation inwards (not that there have not always been internal exploitations) will require a direct attack on the American labor movement, the one institution of power which could stand in the way. First, there must be a relatively high margin of unemployment, both in order to put labor "in its place" and because of the stress on automation required in the new situation. Second, the political power of labor must be undercut, which means imposing legal and economic restrictions on the right to strike and forming social coalitions which will isolate organized labor. Isolating labor politically could be aided by the strong prejudice in many sectors of American society against the labor movement, as well as by the dichotomy between producer and consumer politics. (A 1974 public opinion poll showed that, given a list of 15 institutions, people ranked labor unions 13th in terms of the job they were doing for the country, while they ranked the military 1st and the large corporations 8th. It is hoped that this assessment has shifted some in the last two years.)

Already business is blackmailing labor in many areas with the threat of moving elsewhere if demands are too strong. There are signs that labor is shifting its bargaining goals from securing gains in benefits and income to simply trying to hold onto jobs.[16] Two recent labor events suggest that a new period in labor history is beginning, one which could undercut labor's junior partnership in the syndicalist triumvirate with big business and big government.[17] The first was the resignation of John Dunlop as Secretary of Labor, because of President Gerald R. Ford's

veto of the "common situs" picketing bill. Ford believed that his
political future depended more upon appeasing right-wing, anti-union
forces than on building his constituency with labor. The second incident
is the union-busting policies of the liberal *Washington Post* in the strike
of its pressmen's union. Neither the black community of Washington,
nor the city's white liberals, nor big labor itself really fought the
union-busting. But at this moment the breaking of any union, whether
its vision be narrow or broad, may ultimately do great damage to the
potential power of the poor, minorities, women, and the middle class,
for it could represent the beginning of a coordinated structural attack on
the strongest potential instrument of popular power in American society.

There may be some danger that big capital will try to appease a
limited sector of American workers in order to apply more exploitative
policies against others. Thus, rewards might be offered to skilled
workers, particularly in the defense sector, in an effort to prevent the
labor movement from organizing broad social resistance among the
poor, the minorities, women, the unorganized, and the middle class. So
pervasive could be the coming crisis, however, that even a strategy of
co-optation might not be workable.

Despite all the rhetoric in the media about increasing labor costs,
real take-home pay of workers in private industry plunged, for instance,
from nearly $97/week in September 1973 to a little more than $87/week
in February 1975. And in 1975, it took more than $18 to buy the same
basket of groceries that were bought with $12 in 1970 and with $10
in 1965.[18]

The affluence of the American labor force is deceiving. Workers
took great pay cuts during the Second World War. Immediately
following the war, when there were widespread strikes, big business and
big government countered with strong anti-labor measures, especially the
Taft-Hartley Act. The image of big unions protecting American workers
is accurate for only about 20% of the American labor force, and within
that percentage some of the most highly paid per-hour workers (e.g.
within the building trades) are experiencing extreme unemployment.
"Twenty-five years ago," according to a *Washington Post* reporter,
"two out of three families could afford to buy a medium-priced new
home. Today fewer than one out of five can." In addition, rents in many
urban areas are skyrocketing. While salaries may have increased
dramatically, the structural costs of living in this society have increased
even more dramatically. The automobile for many workers, for instance,
is not a luxury but a structural necessity in a society where the creation of
an effective mass transit system is fought at every turn by powerful
lobbies. Even good higher education, the heart of the American Dream,
remains (probably more so today) beyond the reach of most
working-class families.

Inflation further weakens workers' purchasing power. The upper
classes, whose money is secure in fixed sources, find their wealth

inflating with the general inflation process. Because of strategic positions within the economy, the strongest among them may be able to further strengthen their positions by gaining control of lesser capitalist enterprises weakened by the economic crisis. Working people, however, who depend only on salaries, find their paychecks shrinking every day.

There have also been efforts to transfer the tax burden of the system's social recklessness down to the middle- and lower-middle-income sectors.[19] Taxes rose as much as 30% recently, the highest single figure in the inflationary bag. The high tax costs are due basically to two items in public budgets: first, the incredible military costs of maintaining a world empire, even in its decline; and second, the incredible social costs (welfare, prisons, unemployment compensation, etc.) of maintaining the free-enterprise economy in a highly technological context.

The strong resistance against transferring the tax burden downward, however, has led to attempts to decrease or even eliminate the welfare programs of liberal capitalism. This leads to a second structural attack upon America's people, namely, the fiscal crisis of government.[20]

While the fiscal crisis appears as an anonymous catastrophe over which no one has power, it really represents the structural shifting of the state in the face of the empire's decline. The most dramatic case is New York City, the supreme construct of American liberalism, for it simultaneously houses the nation's greatest financial and cultural power and the largest concentration of the nation's poor.

The fiscal crisis is felt not only by the poor (who are indiscriminately branded "welfare cheaters") and not only by the working class on the production side (who are subject to unemployment, bargaining blackmail, and union-busting) but also by the consumer, who is hit by price-gouging and regressive tax structures. These new social policies, undermining the liberal New Deal, are unified under the comprehensive program called "capital formation."

Capital formation is the aggressive policy, expressed in countless areas, of shifting more of the nation's wealth upwards, to make it available for large-scale investment in technologies which will employ few people but which will give the national economy economic balance and flexibility in the world system.

The effects of aggressive capital formation are felt in all sectors of the American economy, including industry, services, and agriculture. The automation of agriculture is particularly devastating to one root of the American sense of "freedom," namely, the family farm.[21] Small family farms are being gobbled up almost in geometric proportion by large capitalist conglomerates called "agribusinesses." The result is that the agricultural sector of the nation is becoming a network of automated plantations belonging to large corporations, rather than a land of small family farms.

Aggressive capital formation is the social crisis of contemporary American society. It may cast this society back into what many believed was a ruthless but forgotten stage in the early history of capitalism. Because of this structural need for aggressive capital formation, the traditionally liberal policy of deficit spending does not seem to be a workable alternative for the capitalist class. In its view, apparently, massive government programs of public employment will remove needed capital from the private sector.[22]

Thus, economic life for many people in the new structural period may become a time of "downward mobility," in contrast to the "upward mobility" which many knew before in dream if not reality. If these interpretations are true, the American nation has indeed entered a new period in its economic history.

Of course, the hardest hit immediately in the crisis are the families of poor and unskilled workers, particularly racial minorities, women, the aged, and young people. In long-range terms, those most threatened are America's children, who must build the nation's future. Kenneth Keniston has recently written that a full quarter of all American children are being brought up to fail. The root cause, he claims, is that

> we live in a system driven by the relentless quest for innovation, growth, and profit. . . . But the prosperity of our comfortable groups at least partly depends on having a pool of cheap labor— individuals and families driven by economic necessity to accept menial, dead-end, low-paying work. . . . This is the moral price we pay simply by tolerating a system that wastes a significant portion of the potential of the next generation, lets the advantage of some rest upon the systematic deprivation of others and subtly subverts in all of us our best instincts for loving our children.[23]

As a recent study has dramatically pointed out, although there are fewer children in the United States today than there were five years ago, a larger percentage of them are poor. One of every six of America's children lives in poverty.[24] It is a strange economy which does not make room for children.

2. *Political Life: Drift to the Right*

If economic life in America is undergoing a dramatic shift, then the nation's political life must also be restructured. This restructuring, it seems, must respond to three aspects of the new situation: (1) the centralization of wealth and power, visible in monopolistic conglomerates; (2) the maturing of international capitalism, visible in the multinational corporation; and (3) social protest, visible in many social groupings hurt by the new situation (e.g., workers, consumers, national minorities, women, and youth). In general, such political restructuring might be described as the demise of the liberal state and the construction of a formally democratic but *conservative "corporativism."*

Corporativism means a continuation of the trend toward structural integration of economic and cultural life into the modern capitalist state.

This integration began with the reforms of unbridled capitalism earlier in this century—reforms required by the growth of the corporations. Prior to the present period, however, this corporate structuring of the social system was able to assume a liberal style, many argue, because of the growing world power of the United States. But now, as American power contracts in the world and as transnational capitalism creates an economic crisis at home, the continued corporate integration may adopt a conservative style.

The corporativism would be conservative for a number of reasons. First, it needs to dismantle New Deal social policies. Second, it would probably exclude big-labor leadership from the syndicalist triumvirate of business, government, and labor. And third, the functioning ideology would not be expectation and promise, but a "new realism" presiding over downward mobility for the middle class, growing exploitation of the working class, and bitter oppression of the poor.

Conservative corporativism is the kindest name that can be offered for this kind of restructuring of the American state. The use of that name presumes that dissent can be contained and manipulated within the framework of formally democratic institutions. If, however, those institutions prove unworkable, as has been suggested from within even such a prestigious group as the Trilateral Commission,[25] then it is possible that the system would be pressed to an overtly authoritarian form. That could become simply a more authoritarian form of traditional Western political structures, or it might perhaps turn fascist. In the latter situation, the capitalist class as a whole could find it necessary to entrust political management to its most reactionary and racist wing. That wing, of course, is already present in American political life and quite willing to take up the challenge.

The suggestion of fascism in America's future seems preposterous at this point, but it is perhaps worth reflecting on briefly. The most sobering point is the deep involvement of the US government in the overthrow of Salvador Allende in Chile. Now certainly there were other governments involved in Chilean politics at that point, especially the Soviet Union and West Germany. Also, it is unlikely that the National Security Council, which oversaw US involvement, actually desired the fascist reign of terror to the degree that it has been unleashed in Chile since the counterrevolution. Undoubtedly, most policy elites in Western capitalism would have preferred the restoration of formal democracy under the tight control of the right wing of the Christian Democratic Party. But that did not happen and may not be workable when the social pressures on liberal institutions grow too strong. For that reason, the economic and political elites of Western capitalism seem, by and large, willing to accept (however reluctantly) the fascist situation. Thus, although the elites of major Western financial institutions denied credit to Allende's government because of alleged mismanagement of the economy, these same elites have, since the coup, channeled some

$2 billion to the Chilean government, despite economic conditions worse than those of the Allende period.[26]

Some have suggested that Chile is a laboratory testing what social structures may be necessary across the West, should liberal institutions really collapse. It is interesting to note that Milton Friedman, the right-wing economist from the University of Chicago, has been one of the key economic advisors to the military government and that his Chilean students (known in Chile as "los Chicago boys") are directing the economy. Friedman is, of course, a key economic adviser to many on the political right within the United States. The Chilean dictator Pinochet has recently argued in the US press that Chile is the only way the West can go if it is to preserve "Christian Civilization."[27] Probably few of America's policy elites would agree with Pinochet at this point, but one may ask what would happen in this country if deepening economic crisis were to precipitate serious social instability. The skeptical questions about liberal democracy already surfacing within the Trilateral Commission, convened by leading members of transnational capitalism, are deeply disturbing in light of the Chilean experience.

But let us presume for the moment that fascism is not a danger in the United States and that the immediate political future is simply conservative corporativism.

Conservative corporativism can be viewed as the political offensive, structurally required by the new situation, against America's ordinary people. By manufacturing scapegoats like "welfare chiselers," "greedy unions," or "totalitarianism in the Third World," it hides its real role. But closer examination could show that it actually represents an attack on the political and economic rights of America's ordinary people—the poor, the working class, and much of the middle class.

The economic aspects of this offensive have already been suggested in the discussion of economic life. They include the progressive elimination of the liberal fiscal policies of the New Deal's welfare state. That means welfare cuts, regressive taxation, "tight money" policies, balanced budgets (or even surpluses), relaxation in safety and ecological standards, cuts in education and health spending, weak enforcement of liberal legislation, etc.

The directly political aspects of the restructuring can be seen in three areas. First, there is a new balance being created in the separation of powers of the government structure. The executive branch has taken great policy initiative without regard for the legislative branch, particularly in foreign policy. This has led to conflict between the executive branch and Congress, with Congress able to restrain some of the worst abuses of the executive branch, but powerless to take counter-initiatives. This marks the repression of participation in American political life. The concentration of political power in the executive branch corresponds to the concentration of economic power in fewer and fewer hands in the conglomerate phase of modern American capitalism.[28] The conflict between the executive and legislative branches points to a structural need for the capitalist class to modify the traditional separation of powers, ironically in opposition to the originally conservative US Constitution.

Also, a conservative turn in the judicial system is required to support the erosion of participation and the concentration of power at the top. This conservative turn is seen in such diverse phenomena as the move to reduce the size of juries (or even to eliminate them), in the reaction against civil liberties, in the semi-fascist redrafting of the federal criminal code (S.1) proposed to the Congress, as well as in the dominant judicial philosophy of the chief justices. Whereas during American expansion the court assisted the social struggle of excluded groups in response to the expansive structural needs of those times, it now is shifting to the conservative side in response to contracting structural needs.

Linked to the conservative turn in legal philosophy is the growth of the repressive apparatus of the modern state, both overtly in police and military[29] and covertly in the "intelligence community." The poverty and alienation created by a society which structurally excludes large masses from economic, political, and cultural participation leads naturally to widespread crime and to the growth of a socialist Left, both of these being forms of systemic deviance.

Because the growth of crime hurts ordinary people, there is a popular support for strengthening the police apparatus. But this growth also provides the occasion to strengthen the battle against the workers, the poor, and the political Left, both covertly through spying and provocation and overtly through the integration of police and military functions. This expansion of the repressive apparatus of the modern state also provides important economic subsidies (a market in the public sector) to a capitalism whose private markets are weakened domestically by decreased purchasing power. Increased defense production and strengthening of the internally repressive apparatus become, then, not the bad policies of evil leaders but structural imperatives of systemic crisis.

If it is presumed that formally democratic institutions will endure, it then becomes necessary to gather a new political coalition which will endorse the restructuring of the modern capitalist state. This process is facilitated by the widespread cynicism and political withdrawal within the American population. (Only a minority of the adult population actually gave Nixon his famous "landslide"; in the 1976 election, 43.2% of those eligible to vote did not participate.[30]) Behind the symptoms of withdrawal and cynicism lies the judgment by many that they can no longer shape their social destiny and that present political leaders are manipulators who avoid the real issues. It is surprising to learn that a majority of the American people, when queried about the "real issues," agree that both the Democratic and Republican parties are more in favor of big business than the average worker and also that a majority of the American people favor employee control of US companies.[31]

While no stable coalition of conservative politics has yet emerged, there are social phenomena, besides withdrawal, aiding the political drift to the right. Most social interest groups are still operating under liberal assumptions of a past era, namely, that the pie is growing and each group need only fight hard for its piece. This spirit is visible in the craft mentality of much of the labor movement and in the competitive politics of many leaders of racial, ethnic, or even women's movements. While that perspective was able to function when the system's labor needs were growing, it could prove disastrous to all or most parties when the system needs reduced labor pools.

In such a warring climate, where *solidarity* is a forgotten word, the first visible shift is to "negative politics." No group is really able to get what it wants, but it can spoil things for the others. Hopefully, the bitter taste of negative politics will shift to a perception of the interdependence of struggles; but until that happens, the political Right has room to work. Thus, without forceful and visionary leadership on the Left, the Right is able to manipulate consumer against producer, production worker against service worker, skilled against unskilled, inflation against unemployment, taxes against social welfare, minority against minority, white against black, America against the world, etc. In each case, one piece is pitted against another piece to paralyze the whole. Without a new vision of social solidarity and in the face of disintegrating liberalism, the repressive Right circles like a vulture around its prey.

The important point to remember, however, is that the decay of liberalism and the growth of the political Right are not caused by the fortuitous appearance of evil leaders in the political arena. These phenomena are, rather, the direct political result of systemic crisis. This causality is graphically demonstrated in the area of foreign policy, where the executive branch can no longer muster consensus yet must have independent authority in order to be flexible within the new international integration. The legislative branch is still able to cripple the executive, but that capacity generates still more reactionary leadership in foreign policy. (The reactionary leadership, of course, can come from either the Democratic or the Republican party.)

Fortunately, however, there are some signs that social resistance among exploited groups may be moving beyond the liberal consciousness. While those signs are still weak, it might be helpful to review the waves of social resistance and creativity that have emerged in the United States since the Second World War.

During the Cold War years of this period, it seemed as if American capitalism reigned triumphant. The red purge of McCarthyism routed the enemy at home, and supposedly America exploded with prosperity. Past struggles were forgotten, and the present seemed to become an absolute. This collapse of the critical spirit, particularly during the

1950s, was due to the rapid expansion of the new middle classes and increased opportunity for many workers. American capitalism was exploding in the postwar period, stimulated by the war-subsidized industries which were still busy building up a global military apparatus.

The sense of opportunity in this explosion was powerful. One can understand why many—whose parents or grandparents, or they themselves, had come here from foreign soil or from domestic agricultural poverty, under bitter suffering and even scorn; endured the Great Depression of the 1930s; and then watched their sons, brothers, fathers, and lovers go off to die in war—should want to forget past struggles. The past had been ugly; the potential of the future was intoxicating. Sons and sometimes daughters of working-class families were flooding the expanding college and university system, especially (for the sons) because of the GI Bill. If parents felt that their lives had not amounted to much, at least they could take pride in their children who went to college. Even for those who did not make college (still the great majority), paychecks were growing and consumer goods were readily available. Although most workers still could not send their children to college, and resented those who went there, many were able to buy big cars and little houses with heavy financing. Even the racially oppressed sectors were flooding the industrial areas of the North in search of opportunity. Although neither the middle classes nor organized labor were welcoming them with open arms, they still seemed to find more adventure and opportunity in the city than back in the country. And some few did make it as a small black and Hispanic middle class began to emerge.

The expansion of opportunity took the cutting edge off social protest. American ideologists began to speak of the end of ideology and of the arrival of the post-capitalist system. While still short of its goal, the system counted on expanded participation, not radical challenge. The problem was not to find better structures, but to give the structures more time and room to do their job.

A strong sense of dissent was present for a while in the late 1940s. It revived again in the 1960s, even if its analyses were not always adequate. (The New Left, for instance, was cut off by the McCarthy era for a full generation from the American socialist tradition.) In the 1970s it began to move toward maturity and to regain continuity with the historical tradition of the American Left, reaching back to the pre-McCarthy era and even back to the struggle over two separate definitions of freedom in the first American Revolution.

In analyzing the resistance of this period, we can perhaps speak of three overlapping and closely related waves.

The first wave comes from the *productive* side in the resistance of the labor movement. Set back temporarily by the Cold War (including McCarthyism), it has recently revived. This resistance is seen

particularly in the AFL-CIO organizing support of poor Hispanic and
black workers through the United Farm Workers (UFW) and the
American Federation of State, County and Municipal Employees; and
as well in the growth of hospital workers' unions, the Farah boycott,
the organization of textile workers in the South, the reform movement in
the United Mine Workers of America, and a parallel reform movement
under Ed Sadlowski in the Gary, Indiana, district of the United
Steelworkers of America. In addition, there are stirrings of a new
international consciousness. Perhaps the best expression was the
solidarity of the UFW with Chilean farmworkers after the violent
overthrow of the Allende government. The 1973 UFW resolution stated,

> We note the violent overthrow of a constitutional government. It
> was based with the working people and its program encouraged
> Chilean farmworkers to organize. We know that the large
> landowners in Chile like those in California favor the repression of
> working peoples' organizations.[32]

The adoption of the resolution was followed by a minute of silent tribute
to the late President Allende.

Working-class women have also succeeded in bringing their issues to
center stage in the labor movement. The Coalition of Labor Women
United emerged in 1974, when more than 3000 women from 58
internationals joined ranks in Chicago. Partly because of the coalition's
earlier organized power, the AFL-CIO in its 1973 convention switched its
position on the Equal Rights Amendment (ERA) to one of support.

Finally, small farmers' groups like the National Farmer's Union
have been fighting big business on the agricultural side. As mentioned
before, the food system is increasingly becoming the property of giant
transnational corporations, which manipulate the consumer and crush
the small farmer by converting to capital-intensive technologies, further
aggravating unemployment[33] and ecological recklessness.

The second wave of resistance rose more from the *consumer* than
the productive side. It comprises the variety of social movements which
appeared with strength in the 1960s and continue today. They perhaps
can be gathered under the rubric of "community organization" and
identified by their tendency to address themselves to issues not directly
faced by organized labor, mainly because of its concentration on
collective bargaining around work-place economic issues.

The most powerful of these waves was the tremendous upsurge of
the Black Freedom movement under the cry of civil rights, attempting
to turn back the counterrevolution of the post-Civil War Reconstruction.
As the movement developed it shifted its tone toward Black Power, but
the impulse was the same. Though the movement contained such diverse
leaders as Martin Luther King, Jr. and Malcolm X, the tragic
assassinations of both men were seen as a double blow to a single force.

Other ethnic groups also began to organize along the model of the
Black Freedom movement. The Chicano movement emerged with a

range of leaders from César Chávez to Corky González. Puerto Rican consciousness was heightened, and the Puerto Rican Socialist Party made an important strategic decision to begin organizing within the continental United States as well as in Puerto Rico itself. The Native American movement revived and soon became an important cultural force challenging the dominant values of the West. Similarly, white subcultures—like Appalachian whites and later Catholic white ethnics—began to organize.

Too often community groups wanted only a piece of the pie. Supported in many cases by government funding under the Office of Economic Opportunity (OEO), or later by capitalist foundations, they accepted the official ideology that the capitalist system was infinitely expandable. Some even spoke of Black Capitalism. With the crushing of the self-determination philosophy of OEO by the Green Amendment, and the subsequent whittling down of programs, it became clear that, for the moment at least, the system was not infinitely expandable. As the old frontiers were closing, John F. Kennedy had stirred hearts with the promise of a "New Frontier." When it failed to emerge, Lyndon Johnson had tried to turn the nation creatively away from frontiers entirely and inward instead to a "Great Society" which could afford both "guns and butter." Now it becomes clear that not only is there no new frontier, there is no great society within.

As a result of disillusionment with these struggles, many sectors of American society (even middle income) engaged in a profound reassessment of national purpose and national institutions. The most powerful impetus for this reassessment was the brutal and tragic war in Southeast Asia, perhaps the worst blasphemy heaped by the elites upon American democracy. Only the combined resistance of the Vietnamese liberation movements and major sectors of the American public brought the war to a halt. (The final blow to the American side came from near-mutiny within the American military, as rebellious American footsoldiers turned to "fragging" [blowing up by placing grenades under their bunks] their own officers.)

Middle-income people were also mobilized around environmental and public-interest issues. Concern for the quality of life revived a theme as old as Marx's earliest writings:

> This estrangement reveals itself in part in that it produces sophistication of needs and of their means on the one hand, and a bestial barbarization, a complete, unrefined abstract simplicity of need on the other.... Even the need for fresh air ceases... [Hu]man[ity] returns to a cave dwelling, which is now, however, contaminated with the pestilential breath of civilization, and which he (/she) continues to occupy only precariously, it being for him (/her) an alien habitation which can be withdrawn from him (/her) any day. For this mortuary he (/she) has to *pay*. A dwelling in the *light*, which Prometheus in Aeschylus designated as one of the

greatest boons, ceases to exist for the worker. Light, air, etc.,...
cease to be a need.... Filth, this stagnation and putrefaction...
the sewage of civilization... comes to be the *element of life.*[34]

From within this disillusionment, the New Left emerged, full of
immaturity and inadequate analyses, but—together with the revived
tradition of the older American Left—promising to raise again with
power the fundamental questions. The New Left in turn signaled a
broader revival of the American Left, the third wave of fresh challenge.

This third wave, though still very young, could act as an overarching
political framework in service of the complex and fragmented
movements of resistance from the American working class, both on the
production and consumption sides. The wave may be described as an
explicitly anti-capitalist and pro-socialist movement in America. On the
one hand, it reaches back to the complex roots of earlier American
socialist movements; on the other hand, it reaches out in the present to
those whose anger and resistance, while not themselves articulating a
socialist critique, perhaps might cumulatively add up to that. Like the
other waves, this movement is internally complex, composed of groups
with quite different viewpoints on analyses, strategies, and goals; but all
within it agree that the question must be pressed to the fundamental level
and that it is the working people of America, of all regions, races, and
cultures, as well as of both sexes, who must transform the nation.

Many white religious groups had roots in the first wave (labor
struggles), and many pressed on heroically to the second wave (racial,
ethnic, sexual, consumer, and community movements). Institutional
church support for many of these groups did not come easy; more often
than not, there were great struggles within churches to determine which
side they were on. Generally, too, no single position emerged; division
within the churches over these issues lingered. But we can be grateful that
major sectors of the churches were known, because of their participation
in these struggles, as friends of the common people. While the third wave
is still young, controversies around it have already begun within church
circles. It is possible that identification with this third wave, admitting
much internal differentiation, may prove the test in coming years to tell
who within the churches remains the friend of the common people.

To assume the socialist framework would not mean *replacing* long-
developed traditions such as Black Christianity, Native American
religion, Hispanic Catholicism, white populist Protestantism, white
working-class Catholicism, or feminist theology but simply *linking* all of
them in a mutually critical and constructive coalition of interpretation
and action. Understandably, many groups would fear that their
particular richness might be destroyed, warped, or compromised in such
a framework, and such danger certainly could be present. What might be
called the "imperialistic universal" of the West (the tendency to destroy
the richness of all particularity under a hollow and plastic universal)

could re-emerge in the socialist framework, as well as in the capitalist. But such a happening would not affirm Marx's project, but betray it. The universal which Marx sought is what Gramsci referred to often as the "concrete universal"—the universal which preserves and protects human richness, rather than destroying it. The framework of socialism would have to be the servant, not the master, of such a coalition. Ironically, it might be precisely the religious richness of America's poor and working-class peoples which would enable a socialist vision to draw upon the creative power of religious elements in the complexities of American religious mythology.[35]

Apart from the role that religious traditions may or may not play in the political future of America, the crucial task for all creative leadership will be to break the reactionary strategy of fragmentation and manipulation. Creative leadership must be able to link together in the solidarity of action and vision the aspirations of the oppressed poor, exploited workers, and a downwardly mobile middle class. Similarly, within these social classes, the special injustices that have been worked upon peoples of color, upon members of repressed cultures, and upon women must be faced and challenged. Finally, the building of a more just domestic order must be tied to the building of a more just international order. If such a broad framework of solidarity cannot be created, then probably each group will be separately undercut by the "divide and conquer" strategy.

The need for a broad coalition of solidarity within the United States raises the basic question of how ordinary people in this country view the national purpose, their common life (grounded in a respect for cultural pluralism), and their role in the wider world. The question of this vision is the question of American culture.

3. Cultural Life: Ideological Polarization

Just as the economic crisis is intertwined with the political crisis, so both are intertwined with a cultural crisis. The United States of America, as it enters its third century, is undergoing profound cultural dislocation.

Any number of phenomena point to this cultural dislocation. Family life is shaken by growing divorce rates and by the structural prejudice against children and the aged. The subcultures of the American nation of necessity retreat into their separate identities, partially protecting themselves against attack from the plastic culture of late capitalism but not automatically creating a common vision for the nation at large. The symptoms of withdrawal and cynicism, originally limited to oppressed minorities and an alienated youth culture, now grow widespread across "Middle America" and within the "Silent Majority." Creative leadership seems to be wanting in so many of the nation's social institutions, and the sense of national purpose gives way to confusion and anomie. In such a climate, there is rich opportunity for new vision and new purpose in America, but without cultural imagination the ground is also fertile for reactionary politics.

As the social system moves into structural redesign, a new cultural ideology is called for. This need in part emerges spontaneously from the new situation, but it is manipulated and refined by those who understand the cultural requirements of holding power in the new situation.

There are two key ideological themes in the new situation, namely, "austerity" and "discipline." The first has economic implications; the second, political. Each of these themes can support rightist or leftist politics, but probably not the liberalism of the center.

"Austerity" responds to the economic restructuring precipitated by the need of transnational capitalism to cut labor costs (by automation, lower safety and ecological standards, price hikes, reduced wages, work speed-ups, and layoffs) within the domestic system. It is the slogan to be used to preside over the downward mobility of the middle class, the stepped-up exploitation of the working class, and the cruel oppression of the poor.

Behind the image of austerity is the image of American affluence— an image which has a basis in fact in certain sectors of the population, but which also has been deceptively universalized. Thus, at a recent "Consultation on Global Justice" in Aspen, Colorado, Robert McNamara used as his example of the typical American (whom he asked to make sacrifices for the new system) the people who were buying ski lodges around Aspen.[36] People who can afford to do so probably form a loose social class of only about 10% of the American population; yet for many they are the "average American." But neither people like McNamara who call for austerity nor the social class he described will be hurt by economic austerity. They may have to undergo adjustments—like switching to smaller luxury cars or putting more insulation in ski lodges—but they will not feel the end of the welfare state or the attack on the labor movement. Similarly, those who call for sacrifice of jobs, out of a liberal trade perspective, will generally not be the ones to go unemployed.

There is a special danger here for religious people who are grappling with the area of "lifestyle"—a very important theme in contemporary America. Their searchings may provide the cultural and practical insights to help many poor and lower-income people see their way through hard times ahead as well as offer a personal challenge to many in the more comfortable middle class. But to the extent that advocacy of simpler lifestyles is not tied to structural analysis (and therefore expanded into "structural lifestyle"), it is in danger of being incorporated into the emerging ideology of the controlling classes. Thus, it is necessary to distinguish between creative simplicity and repressive austerity by examining the ideological role of such advocacy against the background of class analysis.

The second key ideological theme currently being sounded is "discipline." The climax of American expansion produced a highly permissive society at home. This new permissiveness was disturbing to the more traditional sectors of society, as well as to the old working classes for whom discipline was a weapon of economic defense. The New Left, which emerged in the 1960s primarily out of affluent classes, linked social rebellion to social permissiveness (and, at times, even to promiscuity). In part, their behavior analysis unmasked repressive aspects of sexuality, but it also generated a new sexual exploitation and political paralysis. In the late 1960s, there was a legitimate reaction against permissiveness from broad sectors of society; in the 1970s, there began a reaffirmation of social discipline, manifested in such diverse phenomena as child-rearing practices and the penal system.

The danger, however, is that the hunger for discipline can be manipulated ideologically to discourage creative self-discipline and to impose instead repressive external discipline (both personal and social). Thus, the call for more police protection against crime can be used to justify the creation of a more repressive state apparatus in general, which could be used against other sectors of the community. To the degree that the instruments of discipline are not tied to grassroots' accountability (community control), the new discipline will be repressive. It will be used against the poor, against the labor movement, and against social protest. There is certainly need for more discipline in society; but if this discipline is to be creative, it must be initiated from within the group which undergoes discipline and designed to give that group more social power.

Whether the cultural consciousness of America's ordinary people will appropriate the themes of austerity and discipline in a creative way, or whether people find themselves pitted against each other by reactionary manipulation may depend a great deal on what happens in America's cultural institutions.

By *cultural institutions* is meant the arts, media, education, and religion. Clearly, in much of the structure of these institutions there is little popular accountability. The "high arts" service the cultural needs of an elite social class and functionally reinforce the supposed superiority of that class. The "popular arts" are constantly exploited by commercial co-optation through consumerism and by the manipulative power of entertainment entrepreneurs. The media are increasingly the private property of the wealthy centers of power in our society. So often they distort the story of our society by stereotyping or sensationalizing the struggles of ordinary people, while protecting the social power of the class which owns the media. Education has become a national system remote from community control and stratified into increasingly rigid class tracks. Even organized religion seems to be speaking with little creativity to the hopes and fears of the nation's ordinary people.

The erosion of popular control over cultural institutions may be due to two structural factors.

First, the dynamic life of modern capitalism, with its tendency toward individual mobility and alienated individualism, has undermined the foundation of community across the land and, therefore, the foundation of community control. In the few areas where community life remains, like old city neighborhoods, the positive aspects of that experience are little appreciated by outsiders.

Second, responsibility for initiation and judgment in all cultural institutions is increasingly granted only to technocrats, who have passed through a long process of ritualistic certification in their respective areas of specialization. The creativity and contribution of those who have not passed through a similar precise educational certification is then repressed and even ridiculed. Competence frequently becomes identified with the ability to manipulate the specialized jargon of the technical field. The net effect of specialized training for the cultural technocrats, however, is precisely to insulate them from popular language, popular perceptions, popular aspirations, and popular feelings. As a result, cultural institutions collapse into instrumental rationality; meaning recedes before technique; and the institutions repress rather than support popular culture.

The late Italian Marxist Antonio Gramsci developed the interesting theory that the controlling social classes maintain their power not first by politics and force (although these instruments are available), but by "cultural hegemony."[37] By controlling cultural institutions which condition social imagination, elites are able to build a network of perceptions and judgments which paralyze and divide a society's ordinary people. According to Gramsci, this process is fostered not by crude conspiracy but out of the apparently noble desire of the classes of wealth and power to contribute to the general culture. In our own country, for example, some of the major capitalist foundations moved aggressively into areas of culture precisely when popular culture was most hostile to unbridled capitalist power. More recently, the black thinker Robert Allen has suggested that major foundations deliberately set out to co-opt and manipulate the Black Power movement of the 1960s.[38] Because of their financial power, the foundations can subtly shape movements through manipulation of grants. Those who are amenable to the shaping process are rewarded (sometimes despite their "militant rhetoric"), while those who resist are marginalized. The foundations, in cooperation with government policy (which they often help shape), now play a role in all cultural institutions—universities and education generally, media, the arts—and, increasingly, religion. In addition, their influence is strong in determining what can and cannot happen in a broad range of social movements from radical or ethnic groups to public- or community-interest groups.

In recent times, however, as the general social crisis grows and the capitalist class as a whole is pressured toward more reactionary policies, the manipulative role of many cultural institutions becomes visible. Few people in the society today trust the press. There is growing hostility against the educational system. The commercial arts have become wearisome for many. And even religious institutions begin to feel a new alienation from their old constituencies.

In such an environment, the demand for popular accountability may grow, as well might the creation of networks of alternative cultural institutions. But because it is unlikely that alternative institutions can replace the dominant ones, the cultural strategy for most groups will probably be to act as parallel pressure groups which push for popular accountability within the dominant institutions. Should such groups, however, actually challenge the "cultural hegemony" of the controlling classes, the success may push elites to abandon cultural-control strategies and opt instead for controlling the society more directly by force. The latter strategy would mean increased censorship in all cultural life.

Yet the struggle over cultural themes, which is really the struggle over how we look at each other and our social history, could prove a creative element in the broader social scale.

Finally, there is evidence that overtly ideological struggle may become central in the cultural life of the United States. As the liberal center is eroding (or redefining itself in more conservative terms), the political struggle will probably polarize more around Left and Right wings. In such an environment, ideology becomes transparent.

There was a time in the United States when the intellectual elite told us we had come upon the "end of ideology"—upon a postindustrial system the benefits of which were infinitely expandable while class struggle was vanishing. For a while the word *capitalism* was seldom heard, while the word *socialism* seemed irrelevant. Even today, some suggest that the question of capitalism versus socialism is really a 19th-century construct, with little meaning for today. One group, however, which apparently does not perceive this "irrelevance" is the class of American capitalists.

A number of recent phenomena suggest that an ideological offensive, overtly defending capitalism, is just beginning to take shape. *Time* magazine recently devoted a cover-feature story to the question, "Can capitalism survive?" [39] In 1975, Tiffany's, Chase, and Mobil ran large ads defending capitalism and the free-enterprise system. Similarly, the Advertising Council of America embarked on a mass public-education campaign of the free-enterprise system. [40] Finally, Disney and Exxon have formed a joint agreement to produce a series of high-school textbooks defending the free-enterprise system in energy production. [41] Ideological controversy, rather than becoming blurred, will probably get sharper.

In conclusion, it seems clear that the functional restructuring of American capitalism within the larger transnational capitalist system is creating a structural crisis in the economic, political, and cultural life of domestic society. Where this crisis will lead us is a haunting question.

C. Projections: Facing the Future

Projecting the future is always an extremely precarious exercise and any number of forces or events can intervene to alter drastically any predictions. With that in mind, we might risk looking at two hypothetical poles, toward either of which the American nation might lead.

The first pole has been described as the fresh triumph of capitalist social relations in the new structural situation. Triumphalist visions of this sort may seem, at first, quite justified, because, despite continued Marxist anticipation of its collapse, Western capitalism has survived with considerable maneuverability and seeming adaptability through many earlier crises. Even so, there is reason to believe that the present crisis, tied as it is to the general decline of Western predominance, is unique. A capitalism which weathers this storm would probably have to become more exploitative of its own people.

Samir Amin, an Egyptian Marxist who has tried to analyze the process of capital accumulation on a global scale, suggests that the society will be forced to move toward some form of Orwell's 1984.[42] He then proposes two variants of this model—which he calls 1984A and 1984B—but also allows for a combination of the two.

The 1984A variant is seen as continuing the present directions of redesigning the international division of labor. The world capitalist system would keep new industries (frontier technology) in the center but export classical industries (iron and steel, chemicals, light industries) to the periphery, because they require more labor and because they are highly polluting. The center would continue to control the world system and would be supported by an unequal-exchange model, in which the profit of the periphery would support the center (a model corresponding to a world extension of the South African apartheid system). Within the world system, large Third World powers would function as sub-imperial centers (e.g., Iran and Brazil).

The 1984B variant projects the exclusion of an international division of labor as the result of efforts to concentrate all production in the center and to marginalize completely the periphery. This model, different from the extension of apartheid, would move toward systemic genocide of Third World peoples.

Although both models are obvious caricatures, they are perhaps useful for evaluating present tendencies. Amin suggests that the A model is the most natural, according to the past development of capital-accumulation patterns. But which prevails would depend on the political struggle presently underway between the national bourgeoisies of the world community.

> A weak bourgeoisie. . . can be compelled to make its own proletariat bear more of the burden. Therefore, the strong will incline toward 1984A, the weak toward 1984B; the new period will be marked first

by a sharpening of the struggle between the central capitalisms for access to the Third World and to Eastern Europe. This is the terrain on which the struggles that will decide the new international balance are being fought.[43]

Whatever one thinks of Amin's projections, it does seem that two variants are available in restructuring, although both seem to require more hardship at home. A strategy stressing the "interdependence" of the American system could continue to tolerate job-export and the growth of domestic unemployment, while imposing anti-liberal fiscal austerity. A strategy stressing the "independence" of the American system, however, would probably lead to isolation from the world community and the harsher extraction of profits from the employed domestic working class. In any case, it seems likely that the United States will continue in crisis, both on the domestic and international fronts, until a stable structural redesign is achieved.

The defense of American capitalism would, in any case, require an external and internal offensive. The new external offensive was perhaps signaled by the appointment of Daniel Moynihan to the United Nations and by an article by Irving Kristol in *The Wall Street Journal*, describing a new "Cold War" against the world's poor (not against their poverty, but against their power).[44] Moynihan, in turn, in a programmatic article in *Commentary,* simplistically lumped Third World nations under the rubric of "British socialism."[45] Thus, the battle by US elites against the majority of the human race takes on ideological tones. "Liberal capitalism," to use Kristol's phrase, can produce the goods and wealth, while "British socialism," to use Moynihan's phrase, simply cannot. The message seems to be: If the Third World wants to starve itself because of allegiance to British socialism instead of accepting liberal capitalism, that's its problem. (The truth is, of course, that much of the Third World, Latin America in particular, is blatantly capitalist and without a welfare state.) The defense of declining American imperialism is then taken up under the disguise of self-respect and self-affirmation for ourselves as a nation. In Kristol's words,

> When the poor start "mau-mauing" their actual or potential benefactors, when they begin vilifying them, insulting them, demanding as of right what it is not their right to demand—then one's sense of self-respect may properly take precedence over one's self-imposed humanitarian obligations.[46]

Such a hard line may not be necessary for long, if the architects of the Trilateral Commission can succeed in bringing some "new rich" nations of the Third World into the Western club. But that is still an open question. If those strategies are not successful, the appeal to American self-respect by the upper classes may run into problems at home, for these same groups are structurally forced to turn the screws on the domestic working class. This brings us to the domestic strategies.

Just as Kristol suggests that the benefactors may have to yield their self-imposed humanitarian obligation in favor of "self-respect," a similar process could be in order at home—and in fact has really already begun. Public services to the poor are being cut. There is good reason to believe that the social legislation which grew from the New Deal on, attempting to take the rough edges off liberal capitalism, will be progressively overturned. This could leave us with a much more vicious capitalism, tolerant of high unemployment and unable to provide adequate social services to the casualties. This is not a question of bad will or evil intention; it would be a structural imperative of declining growth and intense international competition. Thus, economically, the projection would point toward downward mobility replacing former upward mobility, and acute suffering for the nation's poor. Already malnutrition is growing in certain sectors of the nation, especially among the very young and very old of the poor. In the process, there will be a tendency to avoid surplus population, especially among the poor, and to tailor population to fit economic crisis. This tendency is already creating a society strongly prejudiced against both children and the elderly. It will also probably assume strongly racist overtones. Zero Population Growth recently tipped its hand in this regard, linking its campaign cause to the balance of international payments and the control of "criminal" forces in our society.[47]

Undoubtedly the downward mobility and closing out of opportunity will create great social unrest, but it could be of two kinds—and which one it is will probably determine which way the nation goes. On the one hand, American working people could fight among themselves for scarce resources (white against black, men against women, old against young, English-speaking against Spanish-speaking, region against region). On the other hand, the heterogeneous American working class could for the first time develop a broad solidarity and a common class-consciousness. If the first path is taken, it will be easy to mobilize "productive" workers against "non-productive" workers, against welfare cheaters, against criminals, against non-union workers, and vice versa.[48]

Either way, the social upheaval will probably create strong pressures on the state to move away from persuasion and toward overt force as a means of influencing/controlling ordinary life. Liberal democracies across the world are experiencing crisis. Just as Daniel Moynihan speaks of the "tyranny of the majority" in the United Nations, so Gerald Ford warned during the last congressional elections (when some believed that pro-labor forces would gain a veto-proof Congress) of the danger of a "democratic dictatorship." The rhetoric is surprisingly parallel. Nelson Rockefeller, in an address to the 63rd Annual Meeting of the US Chamber of Commerce, conceded that there is a question whether the American system "is a viable way of life" and stated that it remains a question whether "free societies can discipline themselves sufficiently to deal with problems in the long-term."[49] He answered yes to both questions for the present moment, but thereby touched the central political question for American capitalism in the future.

If the elites of military-police-intelligence agencies are further strengthened as a result of social discontent (and there are signs of growing integration among them, as well as of strengthening despite the appearance of public restraint), these elites would inevitably assume a greater role in public policy. Indeed, the role of institutions of force seems to have become central in all processes of contemporary social change, whether from the Right or the Left, across the world. There is no guarantee that the United States would remain immune from that trend.

The tendency to use state force to hold the system together parallels closely the growing drift toward state capitalism (although a non-welfare capitalism). This drift would, in turn, give more rigidity to the social system, combined probably with class immobility (except for downward mobility) and therefore much higher class-consciousness.

Culturally, as already mentioned, the notion of freedom would have to be redefined (and is already being done) around discipline and austerity. The power of cultural institutions in advanced industrial societies assumes paramount importance, especially for religious groups which themselves form part of the cultural superstructure. There is danger even for the more "liberal" churches, the social-action programs or even educational institutions of which have come to depend heavily on major capitalist foundations. At one time this dependency existed only for the "established" Protestant traditions and not for the Catholic church or the more populist Protestant churches. Now, however, capitalist foundations have a broad role in theological education and in religious social action. This involvement brings the very subtle shaping process of reward and punishment, which inevitably constrains the political imagination of the supplicant/recipient. In addition, there is potential danger in the strong tendencies for religious movements to provide programs of "adjustment" to social crises. Elements such as the simple-living and charismatic movements here can go either of two ways; that is, either toward uncritical accommodation to a declining capitalism and imperialism, or else toward fundamental social criticism. Within the charismatic movement, for instance, it would be important to develop the "macro-discernment" process, as well as the "micro-process" which seems to come so naturally.[50]

At present, there seems to be a fresh opening within broad sectors of the American working class to fundamental questions, even to the issue of socialism and class-consciousness. In the minds of many, the American Dream is dissolving. The failure in Vietnam and the necessity of a defensive US posture in the UN have undercut the external aspect of the dream, namely, the belief that America was number one in the world, loved by all as the grantor of freedom and prosperity. At home the revelation of corruption in Watergate, the political assassinations of the 1960s, the clear unity between big business and big government, together with the sense of collapsing opportunity during the recession, have undermined the domestic aspects of the dream. Probably one of the most powerful agents in deflating the dream is the combination of loss of higher-education opportunities and the loss of job opportunities for those *with* higher education.

This can be seen in the new educational policies being worked out by the Carnegie Commission on Higher Education.[51] The Commission predicts, over the next decade or so, the collapse of most private colleges not based on major capitalist endowments. This would leave the Ivy League schools as institutions for children of the upper classes. The state schools would contract somewhat to become the technical-professional-managerial training schools for the middle sectors of society. The universal appetite for higher education would be appeased by retooling junior or community colleges into lower-level technical schools, perhaps integrated into the national public school system, thus delaying the entry of youth into the contracting labor force. Already it is clear that the social class of college youth is shifting upward as a result of mounting tuition costs. Many families who for one generation or two rose above rather poor financial and educational backgrounds may suddenly find their offspring collapsing back into them.

Even the racial struggle seems to be taking class into account, without discarding the issue of racism. The civil-rights struggles of the 1960s opened up opportunities for the small middle classes of racial minorities but left the vast racial underclasses in the same, if not worse, positions. Reporting on the 65th Annual Conference of the National Urban League, Austin Scott noted that at least four of the major speakers

> argue[d] that the possibility of such an underclass, the continued upward movement of some blacks who do have good educations and middle-class values, and the realization that problems can no longer be solved through unlimited economic growth, combined to mean that class is now a more important factor than race in remaining poor in America.[52]

Within the women's movement, too, there are strong tensions over the issue of class. Thus far the contemporary women's movement has been mainly a movement of career-oriented professional women rather than of working-class women and homemakers. The startling defeat of the Equal Rights Amendment in New York, precisely by this latter group, has given more credibility to those in the women's movement who take the class factor seriously. As in the case of the black movement, there is no indication at all that access to power by upwardly mobile professional sectors will change the situation of poor and working-class women. While few would maintain that the class factor renders race or sex insignificant, many are beginning to see that action and reflection around the race and sex factors must take into account the class factor.

Further, there seems to be a fresh and growing sense of coalition-building among groups formerly polarized along lines of race, language, culture, or internal class stratification. One factor assisting this bridge-building process is undoubtedly women's leadership. Women from different sectors of the heterogeneous American working class seem better at building bridges throughout that heterogeneity. It may be, then, that the women's movement could prove an important internal network for creating linkages within the fragmented American working class.

This growing sense of social class and the collapse of the dominant definition of the American Dream create great opportunity for political and religious searching within the broad and complex American working class. The danger, however, may be that such work would prove so threatening to the social classes which presently hold power and/or privilege that state force would be used to repress those who fertilize the imagination and attempt to organize the power of the American working class.

Within such conflict, religious groups must be aware of their tendencies not to "take sides" in strong social-conflict issues and to withdraw from sources of tension. Following such predilections, they would legitimate the existing situation and spontaneously produce pastoral strategies of accommodation. Critical religious groups, on the other hand, must beware lest they produce only great outrage and little insight. So doing, they could easily fail to link themselves to a broad popular base and to institutional mediation, thereby replacing prophecy with eccentricity.

The second pole to which the social system could head is, of course, a *socialist direction*. The current discussions of American socialism are still too immature to describe what might be an "American model," but it is an alternative which must be carefully examined. For many, it is the alternative toward which the working class of this nation, slowly or rapidly, with clarity or fuzziness, continuously pushes.

Consistent with the Christian belief that suffering is the source of redemption, exploited groups are making a major impact on the critical retrieval of the Christian tradition out of the broad crisis of Western capitalism. Afro-American, Asian American, and Hispanic American Christianity powerfully raise racism as a core issue of faith in the modern world. Radical Latin American Christianity, as well as major leftist Christian movements in Europe and North America, are raising the issue of class exploitation as equally central. Feminist theology raises the central issue of sexism. The Native American religious traditions radically challenge, be it through Christian expression or not, the Western rape of the earth and the consequent loss of the religious mystery flowing from ecological relationships. Third World Christianity in general—be it African, Asian, or Latin American—raises the issue of imperialism. It could be that some appropriation of the Marxist tradition will provide a framework within which each of these powerful streams of insight can understand their mutual enrichment. If that occurs, then the cumulative retrieval of the core Christian tradition would point toward a fundamental critique of the structures of capitalism and toward some generalized legitimation of socialist tendencies.

Of course, such legitimation would not portray socialism as an absolute utopia, nor as an eschatological realization of the Kingdom of God. It would simply suggest that, while not perfect, socialism might be structurally preferable to the current situation. Whether such a judgment is wise or not probably constitutes the most overarching question for Christians of this country and of the whole world, as we grapple with the Spirit of God in discerning the signs of the times.

The fruit of this discernment process may prove a significant factor in determining toward which pole the American Journey will head in the present crisis. It may also prove an important ingredient in finally answering the as-yet-unanswered questions of the two definitions of freedom—property rights or human rights—which two revolutions so far in the American Journey have yet to settle. The closing of the frontier, the retreat of American imperialism, and the decline of economic expansion may be setting the stage for a clear choice one way or the other.

IV. Conclusion

Thus we see one possible interpretation of the American Journey, which now enters its third century.

A fragile nation of small but liberated colonies nestled along the Atlantic coast grew in the short space of 200 years to become the greatest power in the world. The driving energy of that growth, and the benefit which it brought to many people, frequently blinded us as a nation to the failures which accompanied America's rise to power. Despite the empire's expansion, well known to many across the world, few of us at home even knew that an American empire existed. And surely, if it were an empire, it was culturally different from others. The British before us were proud of their empire, while Americans have trouble believing that theirs even existed. Similarly, to domestic exploitation of racial and cultural minorities, of women, and even of the white working class, many of us were blind. Have not the minorities made great gains? Are not American workers the best paid in the world? Have not few women in the world the freedom that American women have? And has not America sacrificed itself to save the world? These are frequent challenges thrown out to those asking deep questions about life in America.

Such challenges are raised not only by the powerful but also by America's ordinary people, frequently themselves in struggle; but so often they are the defense mechanisms of social groups trying to protect their relative advantage over even more-exploited groups. Here is precisely the social flaw of the American experience—the division into hostile pieces, each pitted against the other. Surely none of us wants to crush the richness of so many pieces, but the question is how to fit the pieces together. Is there or will there be a common vision which will protect each of the pieces and enable them all to stand in solidarity against a threat to any one piece? Or will they be divided one against another to guarantee control by those who are not friends of ordinary Americans?

And so there seem to be two important lessons which can be taken from this passage once again through the American Journey.

First, the inevitable fragmentation of the pieces has been one of the main structural reasons why major injustices have been able to be perpetuated in our history. Such fragmentation includes the splitting of our self-interest as a nation from our self-interest as a member of the full human family, as well as our splintering into races, cultures, interest groups, sexes, regions, labor markets, and status groups. The solution is not to end all difference in America but to support each other in our difference. This is an old theme in American history, but unfortunately one which has been too little lived. *E Pluribus Unum*, it says on the great shield—"From many, one." This "one" must not be the hollow universal of the plastic culture of capitalist commodity exchange. Rather it must be the mosaic of solidarity, where each piece retains its gift, but where each piece also gives more beauty to the others.

Second, the need to discover solidarity in diversity becomes more important than ever before, as America moves into the decline of its empire. Where before, out of dramatic expansion, rewards could be given to some in order to keep down others, now all the pieces are being thrown into crisis. In the long run, the self-interest of only a very few will be served by the hostile competition of interest groups among the American majority. This is an entirely new structural stage, one never before experienced in the American Journey.

These, then, are some of the elements unearthed by retracing the steps of this nation. Undoubtedly there are many inadequacies in this broad retracing, many experiences or aspects of experiences which have been left out. One thinks, for instance, of the important contributions of the American Jewish community, whose role and input was not structured into a process (Theology in the Americas) begun by only Christians. But it is hoped that, as the process grows, it will reach out even beyond the Christian frame.

In conclusion, if the contemporary crisis is to be dealt with creatively—if the many exploitations are to be attacked at their root—then we must nourish ourselves on the dreams and struggles of America's ordinary people. If the search, which has gone on so long in this country, is to be continued, it must be carried on by people who love this land and its people. It must be carried on by those who, precisely because they love the land and its people and the wider world in which we all live, are not willing to see its destiny handed over to a social class built on maximization of profit. For in the accounting procedures of this principle, which is structurally unable to record social and ecological costs, there is less and less room for a human world. No, if America is to be America, if we as a nation are to be faithful to our historical call, then it will be because America's ordinary people—its workers, its poor, its women, its myriad races and cultures—begin to learn, in the fatigue of the journey, that we must stand together, in solidarity with each other and with all the human family.

V. Appendix: On Consciousness and Social Change

How people in social-change movements perceive the social crisis and their own relation to it shapes their strategies and their visions for the future of society. If the perceptions are inadequate in any way, the strategies flowing from them will also be marked by inadequacies in action. Finally, if the perceptions are inadequate, the vision sought after will prove unsatisfactory or elusive.

It is suggested here that there are present in many contemporary social-change movements three ways of thinking which leave them marked with serious analytical and practical inadequacies in confronting the present structural crisis of the American empire. As an experiment, we will examine these three ways of thinking, or forms of consciousness, from a Marxian class perspective, to see what that perspective may contribute.

The three ways of thinking may be called the fragmented, the absolutist, and the moralistic consciousness.

The Fragmented Consciousness

This liberal interest-group theory emerged with early laissez-faire capitalism. The sense of corporate wholeness present in the old European feudalism and even within mercantilist capitalism yielded to stressing the part to the exclusion of the whole. Because competitive business groups desired room to operate without state or church interference, it was suggested that the common good—rather than being the direct *concern*—would be the *result* of giving everybody enough room to do his/her own thing (freedom). The American nation, while born in mercantilism, had room enough to allow many groups and people to do just that. Liberalism quickly became America's basic style.

Unfortunately, the expected social balance was never forthcoming, although the damage was both lessened and hidden by the vastness of the American territory and by a low level of internal social cohesion among its peoples (a result in part of the underdeveloped transportation and communications networks).

The philosopher Hegel suggested that until America had reached its limits and turned back upon itself, true American history would not begin. The geographic and economic frontiers opened up empty spaces into which the fragmented American consciousness took flight. It is only recently, since America has filled up its continent and reached the limits of its external military might, that broad sectors of the population find "free" enterprise interfering with their basic rights (such as the right to a job) and that the beginning of a major conflict between imperialism and patriotism is emerging ("What business did we have in Vietnam?"). It is also only recently, after intense racial and ethnic conflicts, that American men and women, disillusioned with their rootlessness, both look back to their heritage and seek a pluralistic but coherent national identity. In that sense, we may only now be entering upon a period of truly unified social history.

The old fragmented or liberal consciousness reinforced the power of the dominant class. By forming selective coalitions, whose composition constantly changed, the controlling class was able to maintain broad advantage for itself throughout the society. Similarly, by maintaining and managing hostilities within the work force, the controlling class was further secured.

Of course, these tactics—selective coalition-building and the maintenance of divisions—were neither peculiar to the American elites nor the product of a carefully sustained conspiracy (although at times the manipulation seems to have been rather deliberate). Rather, these patterns of control have been the spontaneous response of the classes in power throughout human history. The dominant forces spontaneously produced their own rationalization (ideology) of the situation and of the techniques used to maintain control. The control process, institutional rather than conspiratorial, operated primarily through semi-autonomous structures.

The pattern was extraordinarily successful in the young and open nation, where a highly heterogeneous work force was created (Native Americans, Chicanos, Afro-Americans, Asian Americans, and European Americans—the last two groups themselves containing strong internal ethnic differentiation—as well as Puerto Ricans and others from the world over). The creation of such an internally heterogeneous labor force was presided over by the controlling classes. It was they who chose to import millions of black slaves, to acquire the Mexican territories, to open America to millions of European workers and peasants.

The class perspective raises strongly the question of whether fragmented social movements are not prey to manipulation, or if they are not at least counterproductive? The "fragments" themselves (individual social movements), however, want to ask what guarantees are offered that their *own* issues, which are not simply reducible to class, will have justice done to them; that is, who is to guarantee that, in class solidarity, control will not continue to be almost exclusively white and male? This is a very serious question. Often it may be that class analysis is rejected by many who objectively should be sympathetic because they fear that that analysis—with its supposed universality—may cover over, rather than unmask, their own oppressions. Exacerbating this fear is the fact that, even today, there is no question but that the dominant voices of the American Left are white and male. "Worker solidarity," then, could prove a screen for racial and sexual exploitation similar to, if less oppressive than, the capitalist "melting pot."

Although this may be one reason why a class-consciousness has not emerged within the American work force, the main reason seems to have been the very complexity (sexual, racial, regional, cultural) of the labor force itself and the vast economic and geographic spaces in which it has moved. If the American labor force has not yet really come together, it could be very much because it was still too fragmented and had too much room. This is an objective historical experience quite distinct from the more homogeneous and contained history of the work forces of other industrialized nations, as in Western Europe, where class-consciousness runs high.

In addition, however, this fragmented consciousness of groups in competition remains strong because very explicitly class-controlled *structures* foster such separateness. Several examples come to mind.

First, national employment policy (based on a definition of full employment as 3%-5% unemployed according to official statistics—the real figure runs higher) keeps individuals and social groups constantly in competition with each other for hard-to-get jobs. This policy has created two separate labor markets, the outer of which can be expanded or contracted at will and which includes mainly peoples of color, women, and non-union workers. There is really no reason why the nation cannot have closer to 100% employment, except that it poses a threat to the capacity of the controlling class to keep workers divided and thus get more production from fewer workers.

Secondly, national credit policies, shaped largely by finance capital (through big banks and insurance companies), decree the rise and fall of neighborhoods and regions (and some foreign economies). The open-housing struggles of the 1960s eventually revealed how people on both sides, black and white, were being ripped off by the red-lining tactics of large financial interests. The same experience occurred at the regional level, as in upper New England, which the shoe industry abandoned in search of cheaper labor abroad. Ironically, the loans which are denied for mortgages, home improvement, or economic development are the very savings of the people who inhabit the region or the neighborhood. (The capital outflow from red-lined neighborhoods is a microcosm of what exploitative financial structures force regionally and internationally.)

A third example is the competition fostered among social-change movements by hooking them on funding sources outside their movements themselves, especially government agencies and private foundations. One of the clear effects of the War Against Poverty was to aggravate ethnic and racial rivalries in the competition for scarce funding. The same competitive situation is created, consciously or not, by the major foundations when they reward movements which do not threaten the interests of those whose capital they manage, while at the same time they leave more critical groups at a severe disadvantage in access to information and resources.

Finally, the complex system of prestige and stratification within the American labor force, created on the production side by management techniques and on the consumption side by Madison Avenue, keeps people and social groups scrambling on the competitive ladder.

The result is that progressive social movements in the United States still represent a deeply fragmented, internally competitive, and externally weak political force. Coalitions are fragile and distrustful. No fundamental social theory guides their operations or outreach. Often when they grow too militant, they become isolated and frustrated. When they grow successful, they often fall prey to opportunism or co-optation. Because they lack a fundamental systemic critique, the movements are beset with a tendency to make false friends whose short-term contribution may be offset by long-term undermining, as well as with a tendency to discount long-term allies who require a lot of patient approach.

The class perspective could be an important counterforce to this tendency toward fragmentation, especially now when the material conditions seem to be emerging for the crystallization of class-consciousness. America's economic and geographic spaces are filled, and people must redefine freedom in terms of how they deal with each other, rather than how they get away from each other. Upward mobility seems to be ending with the leveling off, or even turning downward, of the Gross National Product and the drift toward an "interdependent world" (the euphemism for the end of the American capitalist hegemony). Liberalism is suddenly a failure. The individual units of Smith and Locke have created a social traffic jam, and only those who drive bulldozers seem to get through.

As a result, there is need for a qualitatively different kind of coalition-building in American politics. It cannot be a repetition of the efforts of the early liberal coalitions which said, "If you help me do my thing, I'll help you do yours," but never questioned the pond in which they both swam. Now are needed coalitions which, in addition to bargaining pragmatically around operational trade-offs, propose a fundamental (systemic) criticism and a fundamental alternative.

The powerlessness of the old liberal consciousness and of its coalitions was the result of their dealing only with pieces and not with the whole society. Fixation on the part to the eclipse of the whole was as much a part of the old ideology as the success ethic. It was woven into the styles of social science, economic organization, and political struggle. As the old liberalism broke down, however, the primacy of the part was yielded, and a new consciousness of the whole was generated. Unfortunately, the first tendency of this nascent consciousness was to be absolutist (one part appropriates the whole), rather than authentically holistic (a fully organic whole).

The Absolutist Consciousness

This mindset exists within two separate sides, namely, within the controlling sector and within the exploited sectors.

Within the controlling class, the old structures of economic, political, and cultural control cease to be serviceable. As the economic base becomes more centralized (horizontal and vertical integration) and profit becomes more difficult to generate, the class turns more directly to the state, first to rationalize the centralization process and then to subsidize the costs. As power becomes correspondingly centralized, the old decentralized political coalitions yield to massive national political power—thus the collapse of the city machines and the reduction of all politics to the presidential elections. Finally, as centralization grows, the capitalist foundations take a more aggressive hand in shaping national culture.

In sum, the controlling class moves toward a direct *systemic administration*. Such a systemic administration is not the systemic *critique* spoken of here but rather a more consolidated system of exploitation which, in turn, tends to generate social unrest which must be more forcefully contained.

In the process people begin to feel *powerless*. Where before many groups seemed to have leverage here and there—with a friend in the machine or through a local voluntary association—now they do not know where to turn. At the same time that power becomes centralized, it becomes bureaucratic and anonymous. The lives and destinies of individuals, neighborhoods, and whole regions slip beyond their hands. Small farms and businesses are gobbled up. Whatever accessible politics there is seems either so complicated that it is irrelevant or so corrupt that it is unattractive. Crime grows rapidly, partly because of poverty, but partly out of hostility.

The system has become the absolute, for both the controlling class and the exploited classes. For the controlling classes, it becomes the immediate object of defense. For the exploited classes, it becomes the immediate object of anger. In the case of the exploited classes, however, "system" was first perceived naively.

It became at first whatever was close at hand. For many among the young, it was all people over age 30. For many militant blacks, it was all whites. For many in the anti-war movement, it was all people (including workers) in the defense complex. For many in the women's movement, it was all men. There was a measure of truth to each of these perceptions (as we can understand by recognizing that, in the complex hierarchy of exploitations, certain sectors as a whole did have relative advantage). The mistake, however, was assuming that any sector as a whole had control. In fact, all people over 30 did not. All whites had not designed the slave system and the two labor markets; rather both were the design of the controlling classes. All defense workers were not in favor of war; it was the controlling classes which designed the limited employment structures. All men had not designed the nuclear family and its aggravation of women's oppression under the bourgeois experience; it was a product of the free market of the capitalist system.

The strength of absolutizing these separate issues, particularly racism, sexism, and imperialism, lay in breaking the constraints of the old liberal perceptions and coalitions. Attempting to understand the peculiar individuality of each oppressed group and do justice to its demands, these movements at least pushed the analysis to a much deeper level.

The weakness, however, was that the most creative social-change forces were left severely isolated within themselves, each with a tendency to absolutize its own issue. The major social forces thus polarized were the race/culture national movements, the women's movement, the anti-imperialist movement (an expansion of the antiwar movement), the labor movement, and the consumer movement (including any number of elements such as community organization, public interest, and ecology). The absence of a viable political framework which could bring them together was revealed in the crisis of the Democratic Party (organized on the old liberal interest-group model of coalition) which in turn gave Nixon a free ticket to the presidency.

As these movements matured, however, a recognition of complexity grew. In a vague way, oppressions came to be understood as both *overlapping* and *hierarchical.* Where they were overlapping, the recognition proved mutually reinforcing, as for example in the case of black working-class women. The hierarchical ordering, however, was more complex; this was so because within one absolute the victims may speak with all the righteousness of the oppressed, while within another absolute, they suddenly find themselves located on the oppressors' side. The emergence of the women's movement within the New Left of the 1960s, for instance, took a lot of wind out of the sails of self-righteous male radicals.

The hierarchy of oppressions, when not consciously understood, tends to support those at the top by displacing frustration downward. Male white workers, for instance, however oppressed they were by big capital, could boss their wives and scorn blacks in order to vent their anger. Of course, this is not to say that all or even most white male workers are more racist and sexist than higher reaches of society. There may be some reason to suggest that in the honesty and openness of whatever racist or sexist hostility they express, they may actually be less racist and sexist than more patronizing and manipulative sectors. In challenges to groups within the complexity, however, it could prove very important to distinguish carefully how much blame is due them personally and how much is owed to the structural situation in which they find themselves. Whether this distinction is made could determine whether their response will be hostility or solidarity.

In the process of disintegration, as the controlling classes became more systemically centralized in their operation and the distinct exploited sectors became more polarized, a third response to the situation emerged out of the background where it had always lingered.

The Moralistic Consciousness

In this tendency there are two separate expressions, one which denies structures and the other which denies history.

The anti-structural moralism dilutes and diffuses responsibility. All are guilty (and therefore none) and a general repentance (shallow) is called for. The real enemies are thereby hidden, and the structures of injustice which support their interests are protected.

There is some truth, however, in the perceptions/conclusions of this moralistic consciousness, for while the structures have been created by the controlling class, many others have gained relative advantage from them; responsibility, therefore, is fairly generalized somewhat beyond the controlling classes. But this consciousness fails to recognize that there are distinct degrees of responsibility, especially between those who control structures and those who gain relative advantage from them.

The anti-historical moralistic consciousness sees the present moment as an absolute, the time of total decision or total corruption. This perception gives a heightened eschatological note to the challenge, but also makes the burden historically unbearable. It renders urgent demands impossible of fulfillment and transmits them into substitutes for long-range strategies. By placing all demands within the present moment, it shuts out the power of historical continuity, the forces of which were operative before and will be after. As a result, the past is not looked to for guidance (except in a selective or mystified way), nor is serious change (as opposed to eschatological projections) really expected.

The truth apprehended by this second moralism is that the present is truly a moment of critical decision and that the decision will make a difference. The weakness of the moralistic consciousness, however, is its failure to see the decision of the present within the historical project of past decisions, the creative force of which is still alive.

Both moralisms absolve their proponents and hearers from real action, one by eliminating a concrete enemy, the other by eliminating concrete hope.

These moralisms operate both in the religious and political spheres. The anti-structural moralism leans toward the Right, while the anti-historical one leans toward the Left. From the Right come shallow campaigns of national purpose. The official Bicentennial was full of it. From the Left come anarchistic and utopian acts of defiance which, while offering great prophetic challenge, provide no links to historical movements of power within which they can locate themselves.

These three ways of thinking are still strongly present in this society. The fragmented consciousness tends to collaborate across class lines and undermine its own cause in the process. The absolutist consciousness (on the part of the exploited), while rightfully rejecting the liberal position, tends to isolate itself from class allies. The moralistic consciousness is cut off from the historical class struggle. It seems, therefore, that a systemic class analysis might be helpful in overcoming the inadequacies of these three consciousnesses and in building a new coalition for fundamental social change.

Notes

Introduction

1. For a review of Marx's thought, see Shlomo Avineri, *The Social and Political Thought of Karl Marx* (Cambridge, Mass.: Cambridge University Press, 1971).

2. For contemporary statements of Christian-Marxists from Latin America and Southern Europe, see *Option for Struggle: Three Documents of Christians for Socialism* (New York: Church Research and Information Projects [CRIPS] [Box 233, Cathedral Station, N.Y. 10025], 1974).

3. Dom Helder Camara's address is reproduced in "Latin Americans Discuss Marxism-Socialism," Latin American Documentation, LADOC Keyhole Series No. 13 (Washington, D.C.: United States Catholic Conference [1312 Massachusetts Avenue, N.W., 20005], 1975).

4. From the wealth of material on contemporary American capitalism, see especially the following relative to the theme of this paper: Regarding the general distribution of wealth, income, and power, see Fred Perella, *Poverty in American Democracy: A Study in Social Power,* prepared by the Campaign for Human Development (Washington, D.C.: United States Catholic Conference, 1974). Regarding US capital's international outreach, see Richard Barnet and Ronald Müller, *Global Reach: The Power of the Multinational Corporations* (New York: Simon and Schuster, 1975). For a feminist reflection, see Sheila Rowbotham, *Women, Resistance and Revolution: A History of Women and Revolution in the Modern World* (New York: Random House, Vintage Books, 1973). For black reflections, see Robert L. Allen, *Black Awakening in Capitalist America: An Analytic History* (Garden City, N.Y.: Doubleday & Company, Anchor Books, 1970). For Chicano reflections, see Tomás Almaguer, "Class, Race and Chicano Oppression," in *Socialist Revolution* (published by Agenda Publishing Co., 396 Sanchez Street, San Francisco, Cal. 94110), vol. 5, no. 3; or an earlier version which appeared as "Historical Notes on Chicano Oppression" in *Aztlan: International Journal of Chicano Studies and Research,* vol. 5, nos. 1/2 (Spring/Fall 1974).

5. Much Christian thinking on the Marxist tradition has been influenced by the thought of the Italian Marxist Antonio Gramsci on the role of culture and cultural institutions such as religion. For a summary of Gramsci's thought, see Carl Boggs, Jr., "Gramsci's Prison Notebooks," *Socialist Revolution,* as in note 4 above, vol. 2, no. 5, pp. 79-118; and vol. 2, no. 6, pp. 29-56.

For the relevance of Marx's thought in the American experience, see William Appleman Williams, *The Great Evasion: An Essay on the Contemporary Relevance of Karl Marx and on the Wisdom of Admitting the Heretic into the Dialogue About America's Future* (New York: Quadrangle, 1964).

6. The overall analysis of American history used in this paper relies very heavily on the work of William Appleman Williams, without, of course, making him responsible for anything here. For his most general treatment of American history, see *Contours of American History* (New York: Grolier, Franklin Watts, 1966); for discussion of the relevance of Marxist thought to US history, *The Great Evasion,* as in note 5 above; and for reflections on American foreign policy, *The Tragedy of American Diplomacy,* rev. 2nd ed. (New York: Dell Publishing Co., Delta Books, 1972).

Part I

1. The interpretation of the colonial work force and its relation to the American Revolution is taken from the recent essays of the American labor historian Philip S. Foner, "Labor and the American Revolution," *UE News,* in three installments, July 14, 21, and 28, 1975.
2. Ibid.
3. See Williams, *Contours of American History,* as in note 6 (Introduction), p. 71.
4. Ibid, pp. 112-116, for the following material.
5. Ibid.
6. The Declaration of Independence.
7. The basis for the interpretation of the conflict around two fundamentally distinct understandings of freedom comes from the work of Staughton Lynd, *Intellectual Origins of American Radicalism* (New York: Random House, Pantheon Books, 1968), p. 44.
8. Ibid, p. 46.
9. John A. Krout, *The United States Since 1865* (New York: Harper & Row, Barnes & Noble Books, 1962), p. 59.
10. G.W.F. Hegel, *The Philosophy of History* (New York: Dover Publications, 1956), pp. 86-87. Ironically, Hegel also argued that the American political sense would not develop until class conflict between the rich and the poor and class solidarity among the poor emerged. Further stating that the burden of world history would reveal itself in America, he speculated on a conflict between North and South America. For an explanation of how open space shaped American religious consciousness, see Sidney E. Mead, "The American People: Their Space, Time, and Religion," *The Lively Experiment: The Shaping of Christianity in America* (New York: Harper & Row, 1963).
11. R.W. Lewis, *American Adam* (Chicago: University of Chicago Press, 1955).
12. See materials from The Peoples' Bicentennial Commission, 1346 Connecticut Avenue, N.W., Washington, D.C. 20006.
13. See Richard O. Boyer and Herbert M. Morais, *Labor's Untold Story* (New York: United Electrical, Radio, and Machine Workers of America, 1971), p. 125. This text provides much of the material and framework for interpretation of US labor history. For the fullest labor history of the United States from a Marxist perspective, see Philip S. Foner, *History of the Labor Movement in the United States,* 4 vols. (New York: International Publishers Co., 1965).

14. See Mary Field Parton, ed., *The Autobiography of Mother Jones* (Chicago: Charles H. Kerr & Co., 1974).

Part II

1. See Karl Marx, *Capital,* 3 vols. (New York: International Publishers Co., 1967), 1:pt. 7, "The Accumulation of Capital."
2. This analysis has been made famous by Max Weber's *The Protestant Ethic and the Spirit of Capitalism* (New York: Charles Scribner's Sons, 1958). Intended by Weber as a refutation of Marx's economic determinism, it is the criticism of only a caricature of Marx's thought. Recognizing the relative autonomy and even historical priority of cultural forces in Marx's thought, George Lichtheim remarks that "the whole of Weber's sociology of religion fits without difficulty into the Marxian scheme." (George Lichtheim, *Marxism: An Historical and Critical Study,* 2nd ed. [New York: Praeger Publishers, 1964], p. 385n). Similar remarks could be made on the work of Ernst Troeltsch. See also Luis Althusser and Etienne Balibar, *Reading Capital* (London: NLB, 1970), p. 380.
3. Frederick Merk, *Manifest Destiny and Mission in American History: A Reinterpretation* (New York: Alfred A. Knopf, 1963), p. 29.
4. Almaguer, "Class, Race and Chicano Oppression," as in note 4 (Introduction), p. 82.
5. Quoted in T.C. McLuhan, ed., *Touch the Earth: A Self Portrait of Indian Existence* (New York: E.P. Dutton & Co., Sunrise Books, 1971), p. 117.
6. Ibid., p. 90.
7. Ibid, p. 120.
8. Robert Allen, "Black Liberation and World Revolution: An Historical Synthesis," *The Black Scholar,* February 1972, p. 9, as quoted in Almaguer, "Class, Race and Chicano Oppression," as in note 4 (Introduction), p. 81.
9. Robert Blauner, "Marxist Theory, Nationalism, and Colonialism" (unpublished manuscript), as quoted in Almaguer, "Class, Race and Chicano Oppression," as in note 4 (Introduction), p. 88.
10. McLuhan, *Touch the Earth,* as in note 5 above, p. 1.
11. Williams, *Contours of American History,* as in note 6 (Introduction), pp. 125-138.
12. Almaguer, "Class, Race and Chicano Oppression," as in note 4 (Introduction), p. 84. The section from Walter LaFeber is from his *New Empire: An Interpretation of American Expansion, 1860-1898* (Ithaca, N.Y.: Cornell University Press, 1963), p. 18.
13. The classic sources for a Marxist interpretation of imperialism are J. A. Hobson, *Imperialism* (1902) (Ann Arbor, Mich.: University of Michigan Press, 1965), and Vladimir I. Lenin, *Imperialism: The Highest Stage of Capitalism* (1916) (New York: International Publishers Co., 1969).

   Non-Marxist accounts of imperialism can be found in Joseph A. Schumpeter, *Imperialism and Social Classes,* trans. Heinz Norden (New York: New American Library, Meridian Books, 1955), and in E. M. Winslow, *The Pattern of Imperialism: A Study in the Theories of Power* (New York: Farrar, Straus & Giroux, Octagon Books, 1971).

   More contemporary discussion can be found in George Lichtheim, "Imperialism," *Commentary,* vol. 49, no. 4 (April 1972), pp. 42ff; also in Al Szymanski, "Marxist Theory and International Capital Flows," and in

Thomas Weiskopf, "Theories of American Imperialism," both in the *Review of Radical Political Economics,* vol. 6, no. 3 (Fall 1974), pp. 20-60.

See also the following: For a Marxist interpretation of US imperialism in Puerto Rico, Manuel Maldonado-Denis, *Puerto Rico: A Socio-Historic Interpretation* (New York: Random House, Vintage Books, 1972); for a liberal view criticizing imperialism's most blatant expressions but failing to discern its subtler hand, Merk, *Manifest Destiny and Mission,* as in note 3 above; Williams, *Tragedy of American Diplomacy,* as in note 6 (Introduction); Samuel F. Bemis, *Latin American Policy of the United States* (New York: W.W. Norton & Co., 1967); LaFeber, *New Empire,* as in note 12 above; Richard W. Van Alstyne, *The Rising American Empire* (New York: W.W. Norton & Co., 1974); Albert K. Weinberg, *Manifest Destiny: A Study of Nationalist Expansion in American History* (New York: Quadrangle, 1963); and Richard M. Brace, *The Making of the Modern World* (New York: Rinehart & Co., 1955).

14. Maldanado-Denis, *Puerto Rico,* as in note 13 above, p. 56.
15. Ibid, p. 69.
16. Boyer and Morais, *Labor's Untold Story,* as in note 13 (Part I), p. 138.
17. James S. Allen, *Reconstruction* (New York: International Publishers Co., 1970), is the source for much of this interpretation of the post-Civil War period.
18. Ibid., pp. 204-205.
19. Karl Marx, *Capital,* as in note 1 above, 1:302.
20. Allen, *Reconstruction,* as in note 17 above, pp. 178-179.
21. Boyer and Morais, *Labor's Untold Story,* as in note 13 (Part I), pp. 23ff.
22. Ibid., pp. 30-31.
23. Ibid, p. 31.
24. Ibid.
25. Ibid.
26. Allen, *Reconstruction,* as in note 17 above, p. 158.
27. Boyer and Morais, *Labor's Untold Story,* as in note 13 (Part I), p. 33.
28. Ibid. Also Foner, *History of the Labor Movement,* as in note 13 (Part I).
29. Quoted by Fred Thomson on p. iii of his introduction to Parton, *Mother Jones,* as in note 14 (Part I).
30. Boyer and Morais, *Labor's Untold Story,* as in note 13 (Part I), pp. 102-103.
31. Ibid., p. 89.
32. Ibid., p. 90.
33. Ibid., p. 91.
34. Ibid., Chapter III.
35. Ibid., p. 66.
36. Ibid.
37. Ibid., p. 67.
38. Ibid.
39. See James Weinstein, *The Decline of Socialism in America, 1912-1925* (New York: Random House, Vintage Books, 1969).
40. See James Weinstein's review of *Them and Us* in *Socialist Revolution,* as in note 4 (Introduction), vol. 5, no. 2.
41. Weinstein, *Decline of Socialism,* as in note 39 above, p. 69.
42. Boyer and Morais, *Labor's Untold Story,* as in note 13 above, p. 131.
43. Williams, *Contours of American History,* as in note 6 (Introduction), pp. 384-386.

44. Boyer and Morais, *Labor's Untold Story,* as in note 13 above, p. 171.
45. Ibid., p. 175.
46. Ibid., p. 234.
47. Ibid., p. 236.
48. Ibid., p. 287.
49. Ibid., p. 326.
50. Ibid., p. 351.
51. See Bob Craig, "Social Christianity's Response to Socialism, 1890-1930," *Radical Religion,* vol. 1, no. 1, pp. 45-65. For a critique of Reinhold Niebuhr's final role, see Williams, *Contours of American History,* as in note 6 (Introduction), pp. 385, 472-473.
52. Craig, "Response to Socialism," as in note 51 above, p. 56.
53. Cited by John Tracy Ellis in *American Catholicism* (Chicago: University of Chicago Press, 1969), p. 127.
54. See "Argentina: AIFLD Losing Its Grip," *NACLA'S Latin American and Empire Report,* vol. 3, no. 9.

Part III

1. The analysis in this section is drawn from various materials of US radical economists. See especially David Gordon, "Recession Is Capitalism as Usual," *The New York Times Magazine,* April 27, 1975, pp. 18ff.; Barnet and Müller, *Global Reach,* as in note 4 (Introduction); many recent articles in *The Review of Radical Political Economics,* vol. 5 (1973) and vol. 6 (1974); recent articles in *Dollars and Sense,* nos. 1-6 (November 1974-April 1975); and various articles in *The Guardian* (New York), a leftist weekly newspaper, over the last three years.
2. Historically within Christian circles, particularly in the Catholic-initiated Christian Democratic parties of Western Europe and Latin America, there has been discussion of a "third way," neither capitalist nor socialist. Recently some figures with roots in American religious communities are reviving this discussion, although it has been generally discredited in Latin America and Western Europe as a disguise for capitalism betraying a special sensitivity to the affluent sectors of the middle classes. This is not to say that some genius may not tomorrow produce such a political force; it is only to say that those who have claimed to do so thus far have deceived and disillusioned themselves. Until fairly recently, their political strategy has generally been a Right/Center coalition against the Left. This strategy is now bankrupt in both Latin America and Europe, especially in the cases of Chile and Italy.
3. Samir Amin, "Toward a Structural Crisis of World Capitalism," *Socialist Revolution,* as in note 4 (Introduction), vol. 5, no. 3, pp. 9-44.
4. Javier Iguinex, "Algunas tendencias en la division internacional del trabajo," *Publicaciones Cisepa* (Lima, 1975).
5. Fred Hirsch, *An Analysis of Our AFL-CIO Role in Latin America or Under the Covers with the CIA,* a pamphlet published privately in San Jose, Calif., and reproduced in Tricontinental News Service (TNS), May 8, 1974.
6. See testimony of Andrew J. Biemiller, Director, Department of Legislation, AFL-CIO, before the Subcommittee on Multinational Corporations of the Senate Committee on Foreign Relations, December 10, 1975. Also a study by Professor Peggy Musgrave of Northeastern University reported to the same subcommittee, December 9, 1975.

7. See Jacques Chonchol et al., *World Hunger: Causes and Remedies* (Amsterdam: Transnational Institute, 1974) (available from Institute for Policy Studies, Washington, D.C.). See also Susan Demarco and Susan Sechler, *The Fields Have Turned Brown: Four Essays on World Hunger* (Washington, D.C.: Agribusiness Accountability Project [1000 Wisconsin Avenue, N.W., 20007], 1975). A CIA report prepared for the 1975 Rome Food Conference suggested the use of food as a weapon in world politics, a strategy supported by Butz and Moynihan. (See *Third and Fourth World News Notes,* April 3, 1975.) The report concludes that "Washington would acquire virtual life-and-death power over the fate of multitudes of the needy."
8. See Gary MacEoin, *No Peaceful Way: The Chilean Struggle for Dignity* (New York: Sheed and Ward, 1974). Chile is, of course, the best-known case of political manipulation by US business and government elites.
9. See "Seventh Special Session and Global Social Justice," *Center Focus* (a bulletin of the Center of Concern), no. 12 (August 1975).
10. See Irving Kristol, "The New Cold War," *The Wall Street Journal,* July 17, 1975.
11. See "Can Line Be Held Against Communists in West Europe?" *US News and World Report,* June 2, 1975, pp. 24-25.
12. See Richard Krickus, "Faith and State in Lithuania," *The Washington Post,* January 11, 1976, p. F2.
13. See "Can Line Be Held?" as in note 11 above.
14. See note 1 above.
15. Radical economists calculate the cost of the war in Southeast Asia alone at half a trillion dollars, financed by heavier taxes and a larger national debt. They estimate that this would cost about $9,000 per family of four (*Dollars and Sense,* April 1975, p. 14).
16. See William K. Stephens, "Skilled in UAW Ask Job Security," *The New York Times,* February 22, 1976.
17. John C. Harsch, "Labor Unions: The Unemotional Issue," *The Christian Science Monitor,* January 29, 1976.
18. *UE News,* April 7, 1975, p. 1.
19. *Dollars and Sense,* February 1975, pp. 6ff.; Peter Milius, "The Capital Shortage Issue," *The Washington Post,* July 14, 1975, p. 1.
20. For some early analysis of this restructuring, see James O'Connor, *The Fiscal Crisis of the State* (New York: St. Martin's Press, 1973).
21. Regarding the food question, see note 7 above. Regarding land policies in general, see Peter Barnes et al., *The Land: Who Owns It?,* 1975 Seminars of the Catholic Rural Life Conference (available from Mexican American Cultural Center, Box 28185, San Antonio, Tex. 78228). Nancy L. Ross, "Small Farmers Gather to Battle Agribusiness," *The Washington Post,* April 16, 1975, p. E10, reports that the United States has lost more than half its small farms in the last 25 years; that less than 4% of the farms earned half the income from agriculture; and that monopoly situations (or near to it) pervade the food industry.
22. See Barry Bosworth et al., *Capital Needs in the Seventies* (Washington, D.C.: Brookings Institution, 1976).
23. Kenneth Keniston, "Children as Victims: III," *The New York Times,* February 20, 1976, Op-Ed page.
24. *America's Children: 1976* (Washington, D.C.: National Council of Organi-

zations for Children and Youth [1910 K Street, N.W., 20006], 1976).

25. Michel Crozier, Samuel P. Huntington, and Joji Watanuki, rapporteurs, *The Crisis of Democracy,* Triangle Papers no. 8 (New York: Trilaterial Commission, 1975).

26. See Brant Rollins and Thomas Butson, "Chile's Junta Can Attract, Not Manage, Money," *The New York Times,* February 22, 1976, p. E2.

27. *The Washington Star,* February 22, 1976, p. G1.

28. Henry Kissinger, originally an intellectual adviser to some of the more powerful economic elites in this country, has recently suggested that our problems are not with foreign policy but with the refusal of the American people to back his foreign policy. His solution is a stronger national government. In his programmatic speech "America's Destiny: The Global Context," delivered February 4, 1976, at the University of Wyoming, the Secretary of State stated clearly, "An effective foreign policy requires a strong national government....The principal danger we face is our domestic divisions."

29. It is important to distinguish the state's repressive police and military apparatus from the rank-and-file personnel who staff the apparatus, especially in the case of the police. The latter are part of the labor force and just as vulnerable to exploitation as workers in other sectors. Thus in the current fiscal crisis, they, too, are threatened with layoffs, "speedups," decreased purchasing power, attacks on their unions, political harassment, etc.

30. *The New York Times,* February 1, 1976, p. 1, had predicted that "if the clear trend of modern elections continues, as many as half of the roughly 150 million eligible voters in the country will declare by not voting that they see no choice worth bothering to exercise." In fact, of the 146 million persons eligible to vote, 99 million registered to vote and 83 million actually voted in the 1976 presidential election. Thus, 43.2% of those *eligible* to vote did not vote, and 16.2% of those *registered* to vote did not vote. (*Source:* New York Public Library Telephone Reference Service, Economics Division.)

31. See the work of the Peoples' Bicentennial Commission, as in note 12 (Part I), especially *Are You Tired of Being Played for a Sucker Every Four Years?*

32. *The Guardian,* October 3, 1975, p. 5.

33. See note 20 above.

34. Karl Marx, *The Economic and Philosophic Manuscripts of 1844* (New York: International Publishers Co., 1964), pp. 148-149.

35. Even Soviet theoreticians of the Soviet Academy of Sciences are baffled at the continued vitality of religion in the supposedly scientific age, according to a report by David E. Kucharsky, "The Endurance of Faith," in *The Washington Post,* August 9, 1975, p. A14.

36. Author's personal notes from the session.

37. See note 5 (Introduction).

38. Allen, *Black Awakening,* as in note 4 (Introduction).

39. *Time,* July 14, 1975, pp. 52ff.

40. The program recently announced in *The New York Times.*

41. Announced with the July 1976 billing for Exxon credit cards.

42. Amin, "Toward a Structural Crisis," as in note 3 above.

43. Ibid., pp. 27-28.

44. Irving Kristol, "The New Cold War," as in note 10 above. See also the *Journal*'s Review and Outlook section of that date, which carried an article

entitled, "A Word to the Third World," in a similar vein.

45. Daniel P. Moynihan, "The United States in Opposition," *Commentary,* March 1975, pp. 31-44.

46. Irving Kristol, "The New Cold War," as in note 10 above.

47. See the testimony of Bob Packwood on the Alien Employment Act of 1975, *Congressional Record,* vol. 121, no. 119 (Washington, D.C., July 24, 1975). Packwood acknowledges that a ZPG lobbyist asked the Congress to review the alien problem. His elaboration of the problem, later distributed by ZPG, suggests that it is capitalism and not human interest which is at stake. In addition, the statement appeals to the grossest human motivation.

48. See William A. Rusher's article, "A Marriage of Conservatives," *The New York Times,* June 23, 1975, p. 27, in which he argued for a coalition of conservative Democrats and conservative Republicans as an economic struggle of producers against nonproducers. For outlines of reactionary class coalitions possibly emerging, see William Rusher, *The Making of a New Majority Party* (Ottawa, Ill.: Green Hills Pubs., 1975); Walter Dean Burnham, *Critical Elections and the Mainsprings of American Politics* (New York: W.W. Norton & Co., 1971); and Richard Rose, *Electoral Behavior: A Comparative Study* (New York: Macmillan, The Free Press, 1974).

49. *The New York Times,* April 30, 1975, p. 56.

50. For signs that the macro-discernment process is being taken seriously in the charismatic movement, see William Thomson, "Renewed Interest in the Discernment of Spirits," *The Ecumenist,* vol. 13, no. 4 (May-June 1975), pp. 54-59.

51. *Dollars and Sense,* March 1975, pp. 4-5.

52. Austin Scott, "The New Apathy and the Poor," *The Washington Post,* August 5, 1975, p. A16.